Twitter Me Dead!

What business owners need to know
about thriving in the internet age.

Andrew Thornberry

ISBN: 0646551388
ISBN-13: 9780646551388

Dedication

This book is dedicated to my wife Catherine who has always supported me in all my crazy ideas and to my daughter Juliette for loving me the way only a child can. In a world full of technology, Facebook friends, and 140 character communications, you remind me each day what is really important.

Table of Contents

Your Business & The Modern Web

If you're about to enter the digital age and become an online business owner (even if you still operate a traditional, physical business), then you may be wondering how important is it to have an online presence. The most effective online marketing tool for any online business owner is the Internet and your asset – your website – that connects you to the digital world. Throughout this book we will share with you simple strategies to use while planning your online presence so you can build a suite of powerful business tools that will work with your business and marketing goals from today into the future.

After all, internet audiences are burgeoning. Just as a sampling:

In September 2010, look at the number of people logging in to various sites from Australia[1]:

- Google had 12.9 million
- NineMSN had 9.7 million
- Facebook had 9.075 million

---

1   Nielson Netview, 2010

- Yahoo had 6.785 million
- YouTube had 6.6 million
- Wikipedia had 5.766 million
- eBay had 5.295 million

As They Say, You Need to be In It to Win It!

In order to get the most out of all this technology it is important to know how your online strategy fits into your business and marketing goals.

Planning your business and its use of the modern web in advance will save you some heartache down the road. Some of the benefits you'll experience are:

- **More sales** - When your goals are clear in your mind, you're able to pass that clarity on to your actions and make it much easier to increase sales.
- **More targeted clients** - When you know your market and know it well, you will know the best means for attracting them.
- **Smooth transition** - When you plan in advance you'll be able to add additional features to your website or internet marketing plan without the hassles of feeling, "Oh no, my site can't do that? Now what am I going to do?"
- **Stand out in the crowd** - When you tell your story, you'll be more likely to "stand out in the crowd", which converts into more sales for you.

Just as mobile phones took business and its employees to another level of efficiency, so too is the Internet – in the form of social media – now offering business an opportunity to operate in a contemporary, sophisticated and cost effective way. In this book, we have developed the ideal roadmap designed to take you to higher levels of growth to create a competitive advantage for your business by leveraging web and social media activities to drive sales, build communities on open platforms and significantly reduce the cost of undertaking market research while putting the voice of the customer at the centre of all marketing.

> One of the major outcomes of this book will be to help you understand and plan how you will use some of the new technologies to better promote your business.

One example of a key opportunity

Social media is in our face whether we like it or not, and as a business owner you had better "like" it enough to use its power. Social media is a broad term and includes blogs, social networking (MySpace, Facebook, LinkedIn, and more), wikis (Wikipedia is the pre-eminent example), social bookmarking (delicious), photo/video sharing (Flickr, YouTube) and to a limited extent virtual worlds (Second Life).

Here we deal with the most compelling and the most business-relevant sites such as Facebook, Twitter, LinkedIn and YouTube as our choice social media sites making it possible to get closer to customers and listening to conversations and the stories taking place between consumers. The desire to listen to or monitor the "voice of the customer" conversations is the first step in social media marketing. Twitter in particular has taken this to a whole new level.

This book, written in an easy to follow, jargon-free style, provides a natural starting point for ensuring a common terminology and adoption to increase success in today's marketing activities.

Are you making use of Web 2.0 to develop relationships, communities and conversations? In the age of digital marketing, social media has gone mainstream. The technologically astute have realised the Internet is no longer a static channel of information but a real time environment for social media marketing practice. Web 2.0 gives rise to tools, technologies and networks enabling the encouragement of digital relationships, social storytelling, conversations, interactions and all stages of selling. These are social media marketing engagements a successful business must harness to go beyond transaction marketing for effective online network marketing, particularly given the current pressures of the global economy.

More specifically, by way of example, are you using Facebook and Twitter to promote your business? If so, one of the questions you've already, or will face is whether to promote yourself personally or your company. For example, should your Twitter address be @JoeBlow or @JoesLawnCare? Likewise, should you use a personal Facebook profile to promote your business or create a Facebook "fan page"?

There will be many questions and we will be addressing the key ones. Meanwhile one very visible outcome of being in social media marketing is the icons. These are the icons that should (soon enough) populate your signature on emails, newsletters, quotes, internet articles, blogs; in short they are the signs to the world that you are a contemporary business to – well – do business with.

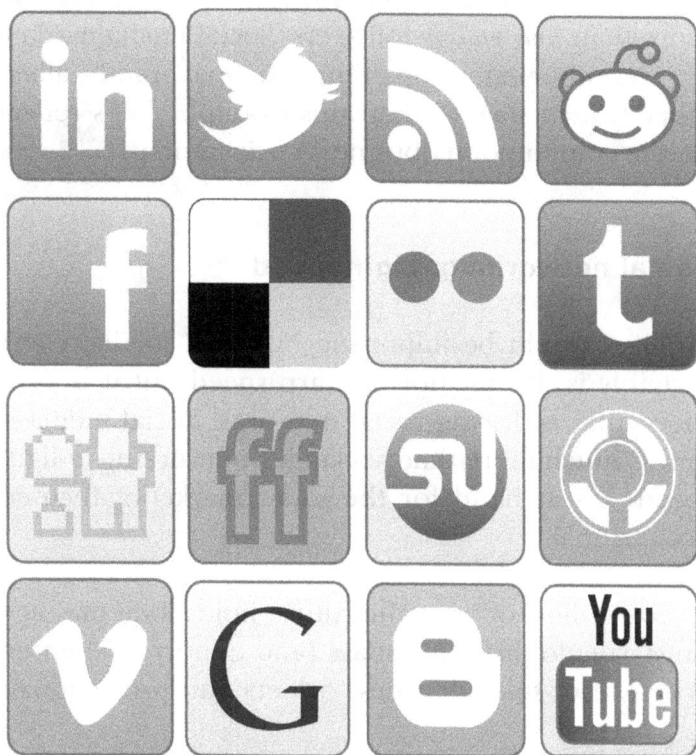

These icons are now becoming as ubiquitous in the digital world as the Golden arches of McDonald's are in the offline world.

Using the power of the web to develop a brand

As trivial as the statement may seem at first, social media is actually following an established trend. According to Forbes Magazine, Oprah has a net worth of $2.4 billion largely because of the personal platform she has built. The Oprah Winfrey Show has 75,000 followers on Twitter, O magazine has 106,000 followers, Oprah Radio has 25,000 followers. Oprah herself has more than *four million* followers. Social media marketing is another extension of this personal brand – albeit much, much smaller than this example. Let's reflect on the contemporary business environment.

Social networking: Lightspeed

Trekkies would be impressed by social media; GenY certainly is. It may not be warp speed but it is light speed that is driving social networks. Social media is much, much more than social: it's networking at light speed. It's at hand for the savvy, marketing-focused professional.

Regardless of what the future holds, one message rings true: to thrive in todays (and tomorrow's) enterprise world, smart business owners and professionals will need to look beyond the glossy, old world of print media and embrace the evolving world of the Internet and social media.

Before You Tweet Yourself to Death....

Having just given you a 'rev up' about all the gold that will be falling from the sky if you get into the modern web, a qualification: you won't find this book is simply internet propaganda (there is enough of that already). Instead I hope to provide you with a realistic approach to this medium – and make it clear that it takes time and effort, there are many pitfalls and some of the latest and greatest may well be a waste of time.

Getting Into It

Why You Should Care

Why should you care? Well, if you are a business owner, manager or senior stakeholder, you should care because in the current age (in fact in any age really), your biggest threat is irrelevance. The irrelevance that comes about because you are not keeping up with your customer's needs.

Throughout history there have been people who have not been able to see past today.

> **The horse is here to stay, but the automobile is only a novelty—a fad.**
>> Advice from a president of the Michigan Savings Bank to Henry Ford's lawyer Horace Rackham. Rackham ignored the advice and invested $5000 in Ford stock, selling it later for $12.5 million.

> **There is not the slightest indication that [nuclear energy] will ever be obtainable. It would mean that the atom would have to be shattered at will.**
>> —Albert Einstein, 1932.

Heavier-than-air flying machines are impossible.
> —Lord Kelvin (1824-1907), ca. 1895, British mathematician and physicist

Space travel is utter bilge.
> —Dr. Richard van der Reit Wooley, Astronomer Royal, space advisor to the British government, 1956. (Sputnik orbited the earth the following year.)

There is no reason for any individual to have a computer in their home.
> —Kenneth Olsen, president and founder of Digital Equipment Corp., 1977.

There are many people even today saying that you can't make money from social media or that Twitter is nonsense or that a website is not necessary for a business. We cannot say that they are always wrong, but we do need to keep an open mind and investigate whether these technologies are right for us.

As a stakeholder in a business today,
your biggest threat is irrelevance.

Who Should Read This

This book is intended as a no-nonsense read for people who care about and have a direct influence on a business. It is aimed at the everyday person. You are not a marketing expert, nor are you a tech whiz – you are a business owner or manager, with so much to do that you have to convince yourself to spend the time reading this book. *I get it. I really do.* That is why it is my intention to make sure that you walk away with at least a glimmer of new knowledge and a handful of ideas on how to put that knowledge to use in increasing the profit of your organisation.

How This Book Works

This is a reference book. You don't need to read it from cover to cover – although I have tried to group the information in a logical manner. Just look at the index and go to the section that interests you.

The language used in the book is meant to be the way I would speak it. No fancy words, no jargon – just clear simple explanations.

About The Author

First, I am not an author. Well, not a serial one anyway. I am not a business coach or self help guru. I am you – someone who has grown a small business from scratch, who knows the problems of cash-flow, staff, marketing, unhappy clients and sudden success. The only difference between us is that my business is technology – and so I want to share with you how you can solve some of these business problems and maximise opportunities through applying good technology.

About Me

With around 20 years of experience in the IT Industry, I am starting to feel well worn. My early years included work in the Australian Intelligence Industry where I was fortunate enough to discover a major security flaw in a mainframe operating system. This launched my career in a way and got me some attention and opportunities that I would otherwise not have received. At the age of 21 I was 2nd in charge of arguably the largest computer operation in the Southern Hemisphere and was also the youngest university lecturer in Australia.

Moving to Europe in the mid 1990's I spent 8 years as an independent consultant in the insurance, banking and telecommunications industries, mostly in the UK and Belgium.

Around 2002, I developed some software called *Comparitel* which was used to analyse telecommunication costs across providers. I moved back to Australia not long after to become a millionaire from my invention. Here I learnt my first hard business lesson – no matter how good the idea is, and how well you implement it, if you cannot market it and sell it, then you will not succeed.

Born from a desire to eat, Yuranga was started in 2006 as a web development company. Growing quickly, we expanded into IT support services, web applications, mobile applications and internet marketing. We now have offices in Australia, Vietnam and the USA.

After having worked for years in the corporate world, I have found a passion working with smaller organisations and advising them on technology matters.

> No matter how good the idea is, and how well you implement it, if you cannot market it and sell it, then you will not succeed.

Email

Talking about email in a book on modern technology almost seems wrong. Email has become such a regular part of our lives that for most people it is not considered new technology. That said, a surprising number of businesses are still not using it or at least not using it effectively.

Do your Customers Speak French?

What would you do if you discovered that 85% of your customers spoke French as either their first or second language? If your first thought is to learn French or hire someone who speaks French, or put up signs in French, then go to the top of the class.

Using the same logic, if 85% of your customers use email as their primary or secondary business communication method, you should not only be using email, but using it with passion! This is a prime communication tool between you and the people who pay your bills.

Email is Like a Telephone

Email is like your telephone. If someone calls your business, you may put them on hold, but for as short a time as possible – right? In fact some businesses have a no-hold policy as they believe it rude to waste the customer's time on the phone waiting.

So, why is it that many businesses who do use email, often leave emails sitting in the inbox for days (if they ever get answered at all)? If you are using email in your business, realise that each time something drops into your inbox, it is like a client has walked into your business or has just called you on the telephone. They are looking for customer service and hopefully to purchase something, so you need to act NOW.

Email Etiquette

Email etiquette is simple as long as you remember that you are not typing into a computer using a plastic keyboard. You are *talking with your customer*. Show them the same respect that you would if they were in front of you. Here are some basic tips:

- Always start with a Dear Mr Smith, Hi Bill etc., don't just launch into the content
- Write in complete sentences – customers don't have time to try to unravel your mind dump
- Use a spellchecker – always (I learned that one the hard way)

- Don't use CAPITALS – IN EMAIL, CAPITALS = SHOUTING!!!
- Sign off correctly – e.g. Regards, Tim Jones, Manager
- Don't write anything in an email that you would not be proud to show your mother –if it's in an email it can be copied, and distributed to thousands or millions of people

Keep It Professional

Have you ever had someone come up to you at an event or in the street to tell you about his or her business and they hand you a homemade (MS Word template) business card, on regular paper that has been cut out with scissors? It provides all the correct information, but looks...well....homemade.

The same applies to email addresses. Using free email addresses is cost effective (free even!) but looks cheap. Getting an email from teddy_g1984@hotmail. com is not nearly as professional as sales@tedsplumbing.com. For more info see the section on domain names – it's not expensive and makes a big difference.

> What is your email address saying about your business?

Email Footers

A nice little addition to your emails is the email footer. You have probably seen one or two before on emails you have received. They usually have a company logo and tagline, and some nice font or colours to the name and position of the person. It's a small thing, but nonetheless a constant reminder to potential and current clients of your professionalism. If you are not sure how to make one, simply go to your search engine and type 'email footer help' into it.

Here is an example of an email footer. Notice that it contains all the relevant contact details, including a website address as well as a marketing blurb.

Andrew Thornberry
Managing Director

innovative web development
expert IT solutions
savvy graphic design

yuranga
EXTENDING YOUR HORIZONS

it's not about the technology
- it's about *your business.*

(t)1300 78 58 07   (f)1300 78 58 09

(e)andrew@yuranga.com   (w)www.yuranga.com

Email Marketing – Sinner or Saint?

Do you get hundreds of emails a week from people who want to sell you vitamins? Or those who are concerned about your abilities in your nocturnal pursuits? These types of emails are called SPAM. Do you hate them? Yes – so do I. Currently it is estimated that 70-90% of emails worldwide are SPAM.

Here are some interesting stats from 2009 to put it into perspective.[2]

- **90 trillion** – The number of emails sent on the Internet in 2009
- **247 billion** – Average number of email messages per day
- **1.4 billion** – The number of email users worldwide
- **100 million** – New email users since the year before
- **81%** – The percentage of emails that were spam
- **92%** – Peak spam levels late in the year
- **24%** – Increase in spam since last year
- **200 billion** – The number of spam emails per day (assuming 81% are spam)

So, if we all hate them, why are there so many of them – why do people bother? Well, because they *work*. Email marketing is the most cost effective marketing on the planet. It can also backfire dramatically if you don't do it well.

Email marketing is using email to regularly keep in contact with your customers. It can be in the form of personalised emails, group emails, email newsletters or special offers.

There are a couple of different ways to implement email marketing. If you have a small number of emails in your contact list, you can send your marketing

---

2   Source: pingdom.com

material to them from your email tool (e.g. MS Outlook). This is very cost effective (yes, free). The downside is that you don't have any statistical information or any of the bells and whistles that dedicated email marketing software can provide.

The second way is to use email marketing software[3]. Typically these tools allow you to choose from or create a nice email template, manage and segment your contact lists, personalise your bulk emails (by automatically putting the receivers name or other details into the email), gather statistics on who has opened, forwarded, unsubscribed or clicked on links in your email, and handle incorrect mailboxes and people who want to get off your list automatically.

> If you are going to choose an email marketing tool, then choose a web-based tool. This means the emails are not travelling through your local email account (affecting your internet limits).

Am I a SPAMMER?

There are a few things to understand when you want to do some email marketing. The first is what you can legally do.

---

3   eg. www.constantcontact.com, www.interspire.com.au, www.icontact.com

If someone submits their email to your business by using a form on your website, you should have a checkbox asking if they wish to receive the occasional newsletter from you. If they select this option then you can send email to them. If someone hands you a business card at a networking event, then generally speaking, they are making an offer for you to contact them – which means you can send them an email. So far, we have not crossed any lines. The email that you send must ALWAYS have an unsubscribe link on it so that the receivers can opt out – if they do this, you need to respect their wishes and not send them any more promotional emails.

Top 6 tips to making your emails effective

1. **Don't overdo it** – It's very tempting to email your whole client base each time you think of something new to say. Don't. You wouldn't ring them up 5 times a day, so don't email them. A good campaign is probably once or perhaps twice a month.
2. **Subject comes first** – If you *don't* want your email to be read, put a subject line like 'Our September Newsletter' or 'Buy our new products'. Boring or pushy email subjects are… well…boring and pushy. Remember, what's in it for the customer? Intrigue them, make them laugh, get them interested. Something like 'Can your business beat the odds?' or 'Don't read this if you have a heart condition' or 'Behind enemy lines – shopping at the opposition'.

3. **Get personal** – With a good email tool you can personalise your email. Emails that start out 'Hi John' rather than 'Dear Reader' have 76%[4] more chance of being read. You can even take it a step further if you have more information on your email subscribers. Imagine if you know their business name and suburb. Your email could start, "Hi John, how are things going at Johns Tyres? I hear that Parramatta is booming at the moment." With this, you have made your email very personal giving the reader more desire to carry on.

4. **Add Value** – This is the raison d'etre of your email: you are adding value to the reader. The main reason you are sending an email is to inform them – based on your expertise or a collation of other people's expertise. Of course, you may also want to sell them something, but this should not obviously be the main point of the email. Write articles about topics that they will find interesting – make yourself the expert and get them into a habit of anticipating (or at least accepting) your regular emails.

5. **Be consistent** - Send your emails the same time and same day each month. Statistics show that emails sent on a Wednesday afternoon are the most read (I have no idea why).

6. **Measure** – Most email tools these days provide statistics of how many emails were opened. This is a great way to check how effective you are being and gives you the ability to test your lan-

---

4   www.interspire.com.au

guage, style, products and offers. Set a baseline from the first few attempts and then measure against that. Remember that an open rate of 7-15% is actually pretty good and when compared to direct mail at 1-3% is actually fantastic.

Ultimately email marketing IS cost effective assuming that you are doing it well. If you are not, you will be wasting your time sending emails that are not read or even worse, alienating your clients by sending them rubbish that frustrates them.

Autoresponders – How to work 24 hours a day and not even know it

Fancy playing a round of golf while your computer sends offers to your new clients? Sounds good right? Well, if this interests you, then autoresponders are the answer.

Autoresponders are emails that are automatically sent to people when certain things happen.

Imagine this scenario:

You go online and buy a pair of shoes. Almost immediately you get an email from the online store saying thank you and that your shoes will be shipped within 24 hours. The next day you get an email from operations saying that the shoes have been shipped to you and will arrive within four days. Five days later you get an email from Terry the sales manager just checking, "to see that your shoes had arrived and hoping they fit well". He also notes that the red colour you chose was one of the most popular colours this season and that many customers also purchased the matching handbag. About a week later you get an email from Terry again saying that they have a very special offer for people who bought red shoes in the past month and that you are eligible, "just click here....".

This entire process was done automatically with no human intervention. That is the power of autoresponders.

Now, while these are excellent tools, they are more advanced than standard email marketing and not suited to all business types. However, if you are in an online retail environment, it may be something you want to look into.

> If you are in an online retail environment, autoresponders should be something you want to look into.

Websites

Do I Need One?

Unless you've been living in a cave for the past 10 years, you probably know all about websites. They're all over the place. There are a lot more than we actually need. There are millions of them on the Internet and it's more than likely you have one, or more, yourself.

At the end of 2009 there were 234 million websites of which 47 million had been added that year[5].

These days if you're running a business, in almost all situations, it's important for you to have a website for, what I call, defensive marketing. Defensive marketing is when you compare yourself to somebody else and if they have something that has a perceived value within the community and you don't, then you're at a loss.

Thus, if your competition has a website and you don't, that will make them look far more professional than you. These days, even if you hand someone a business card, they will inevitably look for your website

---

5   Source: www.pingdom.com

online. This is because people prefer to research products and services online before buying them. If you don't have a website, it usually leaves the impression that you're running a small business from a garage or that you're not particularly serious about what you're doing.

In the same way that I explained about email addresses earlier on, a website is a must. It doesn't have to be too fancy, but it needs to look professional.

Before we get into it too deeply, I want to explain a few of the basics. Surprisingly, the number of people in business who don't really understand the basics of websites and the components that go with them is quite high. Thus, here is a very quick introduction to the basics websites.

How Does It All Hang Together?

I like to use the analogy of houses and property. When you buy a house, you buy a block of land first and that block of land has an address. Even without the house on it, that block of land is at 13 Smith Street. Then you build your house on top of the land.

In the virtual world, it's a similar scenario except there are three components. The address itself is separate from the block of land. So the first thing you do is you get an address and that's called your domain name.

From there, you get yourself a block of land – a block of land is what's called website hosting and that's your little piece of space out in the big World Wide Web. It's effectively, your piece of disk space that you rent which sits on someone's computer on the Internet. That's your hosting. That's your block of land.

On top of your block of land you build your house. And your house is your website.

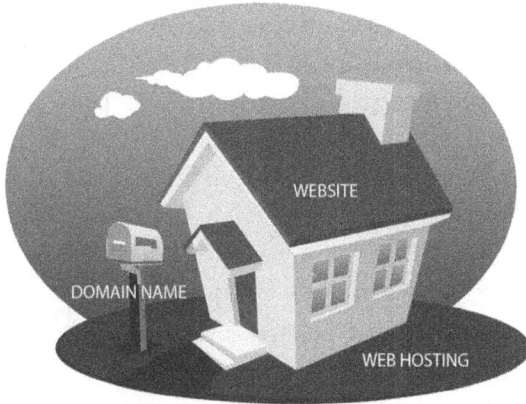

You need all three components for it to work. You can purchase all three from a single supplier –your website company may be able to provide it all for you – or alternatively, you can purchase each component separately from three different suppliers. There are many options available.

Domain names

One of the most important components of your website is your domain name. Many people ask questions about what type of domain name to get, how long it should be and whether a .com or a .com.au is preferable. The answers come down to knowing your market.

If you're going to market within Australia, and you're confident that's as far as you're planning to reach, then I suggest a .com.au. Simply because it's Australian, it's a default location that people within Australia search and it will help with your search engine optimisation, that is, with getting found on the Internet within Australia.

If you have a global audience or play in a global marketplace, then a .com is the one to have. Of course, if both are available, all the better. Domains are not expensive and if you can get them, grab them!

One of problems at the moment with the World Wide Web is that it's very cluttered. There are a lot of domain names out there. And it's often very difficult to get the one you want, particularly a dot.com.

Thus, if you're just starting out, even before you register a business name, one of the most important things to do is to get your domain name, because if you want these names to match it's much easier to get the business name than the domain name.

Good and bad domain names

A name that is too long is not optimal. It needs to be relatively short but also understandable. A domain that uses uncommon or incorrect (creative) spelling is likely to create confusion and cause you to lose customers. Another no-no is to have punctuation in your domain name – a hyphen or two and multiple dots and dashes are all hard for people to remember.

The bottom line is you're trying to make it easy for people to remember your domain name.

Here are some examples of bad domain names:

- www.womenentrepreneurs.sk.ca - Long and confusing
- www.tigh-na-mara.com – Too much punctuation
- www.penisland.net – Though memorable, this is an address for Pen Island, which of course can be read another way
- http://www.llanfairpwllgwyngyllgogerychwyrndrobwllllantysiliogogogoch.co.uk/ - A welsh village website which is not only long, but Incomprehensible

Getting a domain name

Obtaining a domain name is actually very easy. All you need to do is go to a registrar. There are a number of them out there, such as Planet Domain or Go Daddy, which can register domains for you. They're typically quite cheap – a .com.au domain is somewhere in the order of $35 to $100 for two years. And a dot.com domain name is anywhere between $4 or $5 up to $15 or $20 for one year.

One of the gotchas you need to look out for is that you actually own the domain. If you get someone else to host the domain for you, such as your web-hosting company or your web developer, make sure you are the owner of that domain.

To check the details of your domain name, go to www.dnsstuff.com and type your domain name into the Who Is box.

After clicking the arrow button you will see a screen like this.

```
Using 0 day old cached answer (or, you can get fresh results.).
Hiding E-mail address (you can get results with the E-mail address).

Domain Name:              gymbaroo.com.au
Last Modified:            25-Jul-2010 23:47:57 UTC
Registrar ID:             PlanetDomain
Registrar Name:           PlanetDomain
Status:              ok

Registrant:               Toddler Kindy Gymbaroo Pty. Ltd.
Registrant ID:            OTHER 006166141
Eligibility Type:         Other

Registrant Contact ID:    ID00261286-PR
Registrant Contact Name:    Rob Sasse
Registrant Contact Email:    Visit whois.ausregistry.com.au for Web based Whois

                          ID00120656-PR
                          Andrew Thornberry
                          Visit whois.ausregistry.com.au for Web based Whois

Name Server:              ns1.yurangahosting.com
Name Server:              ns1.yurangahosting.com
Name Server:              ns1.yurangahosting.com
```

The important information here is that the Registrant should be you. Often the Technical contact is your hosting or domain provider and this is ok as long as you are the registrant.

There are also administrative and billing contacts that may be entered as well.

When purchasing a domain name through a third party, make sure that the Registrant contact details are yours. This means that you own the domain name.

Website hosting

Web hosting is all about putting your website on the Internet so that people can see it. It's about renting that location, that disk space, on a computer somewhere on the Internet. Web hosting prices can range from very little to quite a lot.

So how much do you need to pay and what type of hosting do you need?

Most hosting for most business websites is what's called shared hosting and that means that your website will reside with probably hundreds of others on one machine on the Internet, which means they're all competing for the same resources of that machine. This isn't usually a problem because these machines are set up and suitable for it, but what it means is that you have no control over the number of websites with which you're sharing the space.

The issue of sharing is what you'll find typically contributes to the main differences in the prices you'll have to pay. You can get website hosting for as little as $5 a month up to many hundreds of dollars a month. The $5 a month ones are typically very crowded. You'll have a lot of sites on that machine, which will make them slower and more prone to other issues. The more expensive ones will of course have fewer sites using those shared resources.

Other things that you are paying for include:

- **Disk Space** – The physical amount of space allocated to you on the hard disk of the computer.
- **Bandwidth** – Each time someone views your website, data files are transferred to and from your hosting server. The size of these files is calculated and accumulated and the total per month is your bandwidth.
- **Email Addresses** – Most hosting provides a limited number of email addresses.
- **Databases** – These days, most sites will need at least one database behind them.

Many people get very excited about comparing the offerings of various providers based on the above information. While this is fine, it's not the most important thing as these days almost all providers are offering way more than the average website will ever need. It's a marketing ploy – they offer 50 GB of disk space, 25 GB of bandwidth, knowing full well that most people will only use $1/10^{th}$ or $1/100^{th}$ of that. So the bottom line is that in almost all cases you will have enough, so going with a provider who offers an extra 5GB of disk space is of no real benefit.

More importantly, you need to be aware of some other less obvious indicators.

For instance, you can look at the uptime. People often don't realise this but most website companies will give you 99% per cent guaranteed uptime, or some will give you 99.99 per cent guaranteed uptime. Those two numbers look more or less the same to most people, but what 99 per cent uptime actually means is that you could have up to three and a half days downtime per year. So your site could be down for three and a half days in a year. This does not sound like a lot but you don't want those three and a half days to happen around the time of one of your annual sales!

99.99 per cent uptime, on the other hand, guarantees downtime of only one-third of a day annually at most. So it's only a small difference when you look at the number on the page but can make the difference between three and a half days down a year and about a third of a day down, which is a large difference in business.

The other thing to look at: the cheaper websites will probably *not* be hosted in Australia. So they'll be sitting on a machine in the US, which may or may not be a bad thing. If your market is international then having your site sit on a machine in the US is probably ok because a lot of your clients may be coming from the States. If they're coming from Europe, they probably have a good connection to the US. Whereas if your clients are situated in Australia, then it's much better to have your site hosted here.

The reason for this comes down to speed and the ability to contact customer support. If you're dealing with a company in the US or India, for example, you may not be able to reach them during your office hours. And when you finally do reach them, you may not get the service you're expecting or are hoping for from a company based here.

To find out about a host, you can try just phoning a few of the companies to test them out. When you get to the "Press one for sales, press two for support" - press two for support and find out how long it takes them to answer the phone, who answers it and how they answer it. Ask a few questions and see what sort of responses you get. It's like anything: you need to shop around a little bit.

Look for a reputable company, one that has a professional-looking website that has some longevity. Ask them where their servers are located, where it's hosted. Are they in big data centres in Sydney, Brisbane and Melbourne or are they in some small location in somebody's office. Are they in Australia or not?

You can choose to pay month by month and see how it goes. It's not difficult to move your website from one hosting location to another so you can trial them for a couple of months then if it's no good, you can move.

Here is a list of well-known hosting companies.

Australia	Worldwide
www.netregistry.com.au	www.godaddy.com
www.melbourneit.com.au	www.webhostinggeeks.com
www.digitalpacific.com.au	www.fatcow.com

Please note that there are thousands of web hosting companies and these are just a few – this list is not meant to serve as a recommendation.

> When looking for web hosting, don't focus too much on the technical details. If you find a good company, with good customer service, they will help you with the rest.

What Flavour Do I Want?

There are three different types of websites that you've probably come across.

- Brochure Sites
- eCommerce Sites
- Web Applications

Brochure Sites

The first one is a brochure-style website, which are exactly like a tri-fold or A4 brochure. Their purpose is to pass information, to look glossy and pretty and to have a call to action – which is usually to make contact with the vendor in some way

A brochure-style website doesn't actually do very much and the benefits are that they're usually the easiest, cheapest and fastest type of websites to get up and running. Of course, the limitations are the same as with a brochure in that, they're just there for people to read and they don't provide any extra benefit to you or to the potential end user.

What makes a good brochure website?

One of the biggest mistakes that many businesses make with respect to their website and the Internet in general is to think that this is a different type of marketing. It's not. It's a different *medium*. The marketing concepts that many of us understand are the same. You need to attract attention, provide a compelling argument and then push a call to action. It's A-B-C and a website is not much different. Here are a few points to consider with your website.

- **Look and Feel** – The website needs to look nice. The same way that a photocopied black and white, hand written flyer is probably not a good promotion of your business, a home-made, unprofessional design for your website is the same. There is more information on this in the design section below.
- **Attention grabbing headlines** – 'Welcome to my Website' – got you excited yet? No, I didn't think so. Your headlines are the key to making people read more. Do some research, find out

what your customers really want to know/see and then turn that into a headline.

- **Add Value** – One of the things that a brochure style website can offer that a regular brochure cannot is unlimited copy space. This means that you can go much further than a regular brochure. One of the best means is to offer free information to your current and potential client base. Write articles in your area of expertise. If you sell tyres, write information about different types of tyres, about what to look for in a tyre, and about the right tyre to use in different road and weather conditions. It may seem like common knowledge to you, but most of us tyre plebs have no idea – so enlighten us. We may not buy anything from you today, but we will certainly know where do go when we do need tyres.

- **Call To Action** – In all forms of marketing, a common mistake is to forget to tell the consumer what to do. Again, it may seem obvious, but a well-placed call to action can make a large difference in conversion rates. OK, so I have read your website, I think I like what you are saying and your offering looks interesting. What should I do? Call you? Email you? Come into your office? What happens if I do? Something like, 'Call us before the end of March and tell us if you like our website and we will give you 10% off your first purchase' will provide an incentive, tell the customer what to do and tell you how effective your site is.

> Websites are not a different type of
> marketing – just a different medium.

Print or Original

In the same way that in the art world you can choose to purchase an original piece or a print, there is a similar choice in the web design.

When you're looking at brochure-style websites, you need to decide whether to go for a custom-designed site or pick something off the shelf – a template-type site. There are many beautifully designed template sites out there, but if you're going for something like that, remember that it's not unique. There could be one, two, 100 or 1000 other people out there with exactly the same design for their website.

If you're looking at a full brand image, it's difficult to get an off-the-shelf, template website to match your look and feel.

I suggest that the best long-term solution for a growing business is a custom website, however it is more expensive. Here you need to find a graphic designer or web designer who will look at your full layout, your logo, your colour schemes, your business cards and then build a website that fits that mould.

That way, it's designed exactly how you want it because typically it's created in a consultative way, with plenty of communication back and forth. Hopefully, this way, you get something you want and that you're really proud of.

E-commerce Websites

The second, broad type of website is what we call an e-commerce website, which effectively shifts the products and services that you sell online and allows people to purchase them.

Many of you will already have done this as buyers. You may have bought something on E-bay or Amazon. com or, perhaps a local website.

The beauty of an e-commerce website is that it can sell your products 24 hours a day, seven days a week, 365 days a year.

How realistic is that? Well, if you're selling in an international market, it's very realistic because while you're asleep, other people can be awake, purchasing your goods online.

In a local market, not too many people are buying at 2 a.m. in the morning. Nonetheless, it enables people to purchase your products quickly and efficiently online and pay with their credit card.

These days, people are becoming less concerned with paying for items online because with the right security techniques, you can make it safe for people to make purchases and also for you to protect yourself.

One of the main distinctions between an e-commerce website and a brochure-style website is that, while ultimately your aim is to sell something on both websites, an e-commerce website is a more direct sales tool as opposed to a marketing tool. Thus it needs to be designed and built differently.

On a brochure-style website, you're looking to impress people, to try to keep them on the site as long as possible to read about what you do, and then you'll have a call to action where the website visitor is invited to contact you. An e-commerce website is a little different in that you want people to get to the products as quickly as possible.

While an e-commerce website should be reasonably attractive, at it doesn't need to be as flashy or impressive as your brochure-style website. It needs to look professional and trustworthy.

Where many people make a mistake is that they try to make their e-commerce website too similar to a brochure-style website, and then when people arrive at your website, they may be keen to buy but they're hit with roadblocks. You don't want people to sit through a 10-second animation when all they want to do is buy one of your products.

You also don't want people to have difficulty finding the link to your online store so you need to make the website very simple. As soon as they hit the site, they should be seeing products and specials. You need to make sure your online purchasing process is not a complex one, with the minimum number of clicks as possible.

The components of an e-commerce website are, of course, the website itself, the product catalogue – typically containing one or more images of each product - the product name, the details, the pricing information, and any various attributes such as size, colour, shape delivery methods, and things like that.

> Don't underestimate when you're building an e-commerce website the amount of time it will take to get your products into the system. It is a time-consuming process, particularly at the start-up point.

One of the issues we strike a lot is that people have an unreasonable expectation of deadlines.

Many people think that once they have the site, it won't take long to put in products. They may have 1000 products, each requiring photos that must be put into a decent format, then loading them up and adding in the descriptions and prices, it's a labour-intensive project. It all takes time, and you need to consider that when you're planning your e-commerce website and your website launch.

Payment systems

Your e-commerce website will also need a payment system. There are several ways to do this, ranging from a simple method known as PayPal (www.paypal.com.au), which is an excellent tool to use if you're in the lower end of the market, if you're selling small items and you're not trying to appear too upmarket. PayPal does have a certain status and reputation, whereby people believe it's for backyard players rather than professional online stores, but this is evolving.

Understanding Payment Systems

Many people really struggle with understanding how payment systems work. It is quite confusing as there are usually a few different entities involved. In reality there are 2 elements that are essential – the Internet merchant facility provider and the payment gateway.

- **Merchant Facility Provider** – This is typically your bank. Many businesses already have a merchant facility. It is a fairly simple process to have this converted to an *internet* merchant facility.

To be honest, I don't really think there is much of a difference from the banks perspective except they get to slug you with an extra fee. Essentially this allows your business to accept credit cards.

- **Payment Gateway** – This is the organisation that actually processes the payment of the credit card on your behalf. They take the card details and pass the relevant information to the banks and the credit card companies, facilitating the debit from the consumer's credit card and the credit into your bank account. In most cases, a payment will take no longer than 24 hours to come into your account.

Most banks provide Payment Gateways as well as Merchant Facilities. An alternative is to use a third party Payment Gateway such as Eway (www.eway.com.au) or Authorize.net (www.authorize.net).

Hosting or Not Hosting The Payment System

Once you have decided on your merchant facility provider and merchant gateway provider, the next question is whether to 'host' the payment system on your website or not. What this means is whether the consumer enters their credit card details using your website or another third party website. There are arguments for each option.

- **Payment on your website**
  - o Consistent look and feel with this option. The consumer sees no difference in the process. They are still on your website and just move onto the screen to take credit card details.
- **Payment on payment gateway website**
  - o The security aspects are handled by the payment gateway. If you're going to be hosting your payment system on your website, then you'll also need a security certificate, which is called an SSL (secure socket layer) certificate. You'll know you're on an SSL website when you see "https" in the URL address line where you normally see http and then the domain name in the address bar. You'll also see a padlock symbol down in the bottom right-hand corner of your browser.

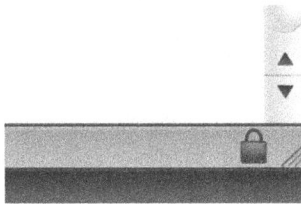

If you see those things, you know you're on a secure site and that your credit card details can't be pilfered by anybody else. Thus, if you're going to be hosting this information on your website, then you'll need to purchase an SSL certificate and your web company will sort that out for you. But it's an extra annual cost at somewhere between $50 and $1000 per annum. This is a huge difference and you need to talk to a professional to understand the reasons behind the price variation.

A gateway system that you can manage has the advantage of being under your in-house control. Once trained a relatively junior person can manage payments and ensure that the business accounting system is brought up to date each day.

Handling Payments from within your website

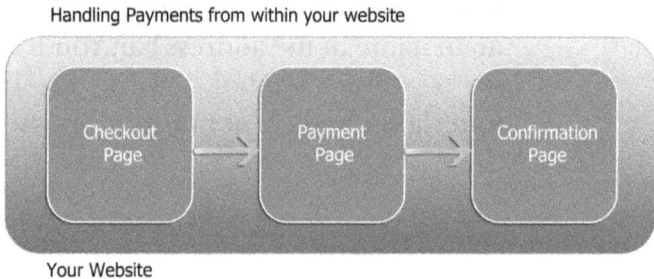

Checkout Page → Payment Page → Confirmation Page

Your Website

The alternative of course is if you're going with your bank, you will actually pass clients away from your website to the bank's website to handle purchases for you.

Using 3rd party payment screens

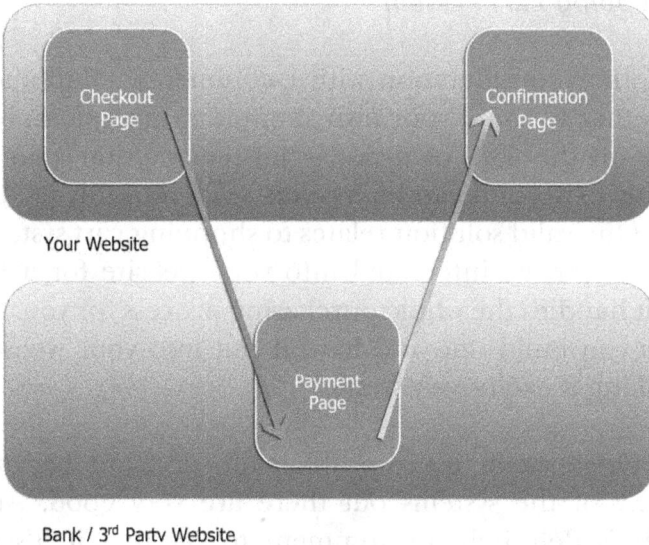

Your Website

Bank / 3rd Party Website

If you're not sure which way to go when you choose, it doesn't really matter. I always say that if you can keep people on your website, it's a consistent process for them. However, there are arguments to say that if you take them from your website to, for example, the Westpac bank to make their payment, it provides an added level and feeling of security for them.

So research the options thoroughly, have a look at the various costs the banks are going to charge compared with a third-party provider and perhaps take into consideration the advice of your web developer as well.

Shopping cart system

Another consideration with e-commerce solutions is whether to build your own shopping cart system, buy one off the shelf or to use a 'hosted solution' that already exists and can be 'rented' on a monthly fee basis. One valid solution relates to shopping cart systems which can be integrated into your website for a fee that handles the whole purchasing process for you. Or you can build one and have it put into your website making it exclusively yours.

Once again it's a problematic decision because many of the systems out there are very good. And there's definitely an argument to say that if it's already been built and is used all over the world then why shouldn't you use it? I believe that if you can do that and integrate it into your website correctly so that it looks like a smoothly flowing system, with the same look and feel as your site, then that's probably a good solution.

Hosted Solutions	Off The Shelf Solutions
www.bigcommerce.com	www.oscommerce.com
www.shopsite.com	www.zencart.com
www.pinnaclecart.com	www.magentocommerce.com

Web applications

This is the final type of website as we know it, at this point. Looking back, we've gone from the brochure-style website, which gives information to the e-commerce site, which enables people to purchase your goods online. And, finally we come to the web application, which basically makes the website *do something* for you.

That 'something' can be anything from customer relationship management systems, invoicing systems, quoting systems. Even Facebook is essentially a web application; it is software for the Internet. There are a many benefits to this. I'm a big fan of web applications and, absolutely, this is the future.

In the past 30 years of IT, software has been developed and installed on PCs with a lot of good and bad outcomes. One of the issues is that every time you get an upgrade you need to reinstall it on your PC. If you have an office with 10 PCs, you need to install it individually on each PC because it runs independently.

Web applications on the other hand take that software and put it on the Internet or in the 'cloud', if you like, to make it accessible by those PCs using a web browser. There are numerous benefits to this solution. One of the main ones is that because it's in a single location, there is no installation required. If people have a web browser and an Internet connection, they can access it.

Web applications enable you to work on your application from home, from within the office, within the car or with a mobile device. Thus, it takes away any problems such as, "Oh, my invoicing system's at work so I can't generate an invoice here and now."

The other benefit of a web application is that it enables you to open it out to other people. For example, again talking about invoicing systems, imagine a customer phones you to talk about an invoice you sent them, to tell you they haven't received an invoice. With a web application-based invoicing system, they can log on and have a partial view of your invoicing system and see their own invoices. The customer can print an invoice off at will. They can click a button and regenerate an invoice, and have it emailed to them automatically.

One of the other benefits is that you may be able to pass off some of the administrative tasks that you would have normally had to do yourself. This is great for the customer, too, because they can make something happen immediately without having to wait for you. For example, in the case of a request for a quote, usually you would have to phone or visit the customer and ask them a raft of questions before you could generate the quote.

Imagine if your customer can go online and answer those questions on your website instead? One of two things can happen at this point: if the quote was easy to generate it could be automatically processed using the information that was given. For more complex quotes, the information could be passed through to you and you could respond personally. Either way, the time taken to enter the information has been done by the customer and not by you.

> Web applications are useful for making your business process more effective by giving your client greater access to solve problems themselves.

Online Quoting

Let's look at an example: A client had and event hire business that hired out supplies for 'the big day' including marquees, cutlery, tables and chairs, and other items. Without a web application to handle online hiring details, the business would require a team of three or four people in an office to meet in person with brides, bridesmaids, mums and grandmothers. The employee would be required to be available to sit and flick through catalogues and answer questions about cutlery, glasses and tablecloths and chairs with the client, regardless of when they came into the office. And for every client, several meetings would likely ensue before all the details were finalised.

A web application solution would involve building an online quoting system along with their catalogue.

The bride can now go online anytime she wants, at home, in the evening or in the bath. She can invite friends and family over to look at the products online (maybe not while she is in the bath) with nice big glossy images and then add them to a cart in order to request a quote.

The consultant is not yet involved in any of this process so the bride can take as long as she wants, saving hours of work. Then when the consultant receives the product information, they can simply phone the bride and discuss the details of the quote, cutting down the sales process time significantly. Therefore, this particular client saved tens of thousands of dollars on staffing costs just by changing the ordering to an online quoting system.

Customer Relationship

Another example of a simple web application concerns a beautician who had her own salon. She was a very savvy lady when it came to marketing and one of her core business strategies was building the customer relationship. So she would have the birth dates of all the regulars who used her salon. On their birthday, she would send them some flowers.

However, it was taking a lot of time. Every day she had to check to see if there were any birthdays, then she would have to call and order the flowers. Therefore we created an online application that she could use to could enter everybody's birthday's as they became clients. The system would automatically check every day to see what birthdays were on that day or the next. Then, an automatic email would be sent to the florist, along with the person's name and address details and a message, which may or may not have been personal at the beautician's discretion, wishing them a happy birthday. The florist would send the flowers out and send a bill at the end of the month.

The whole process gave that impression of being a very personalised service, which is very good for client relations but effectively didn't take her any time at all. And all that was done with a web application.

Whereas typically a brochure-style website is trying to bring people to your website to learn about you, gain confidence in you and provide a call to action to get them to come into your office, an e-commerce website is built to get people to purchase something then and there online. A web application serves a different purpose.

It's not necessarily about selling a product but it is about reducing your overhead. So it doesn't increase top-line, instead it reduces expenses and improves the bottom line. And this is done by cutting down time spent on the phone or face-to-face with clients, providing the clients with a more flexible environment in which to interact with you, reducing staff hours needed to support those clients and, in many cases, increasing the level of customer support that you can provide.

So it's a good way for a small organisation to provide top-class service without the larger staff numbers.

Things to Consider When Getting a Website

Design

Design is really important. You have about three seconds to capture somebody's attention. That's not very long, so when they first hit your website they need to be impressed. They need to see something that makes them want to keep looking at your website and typically that's done with good design, good colour, good layout, maybe some animation.

Keeping people on your site is a challenge. If you want to see the future, watch your teenager surf the net: about 5 millisecond attention span is given to every page view. They instantly get whether they want to hang around on a particular website. If it's of no interest; there's no second chance given. Adults too are becoming far more discerning in whether they want to spend any time at all on a website. For sure, they'll give it more than 5 milliseconds but about 3 seconds is what it takes to look at a site's domain name, its tag line and a couple of sentences at the top or across the menu. But if the flow of information is not seamless, they will close the site and move on.

It's a given in today's Internet-enabled world that all the technical aspects, the coding, the architecture, the page links are all fully functional.

Your website has to provide enough incentive to the visitor for them to hang around and call them to take some action. It must have a compelling copy. The best design in the world won't do it; the latest flash media won't do it: its information that will do it. We will look at this aspect later.

But for now it's important to note that the visitor to the website must get to the point where she sees that your offering speaks to her problems.

Indeed good navigation is about relating a problem and causing the visitor to stay with your offer: because it speaks to them about their problem. They are there for information (unless you're a teenager and want to be turned on by music or social chatter); they come to your site, looking for solutions in relation to a problem.

Maybe they're curious about locating a chiropractor in the neighbourhood who can fix their lower back pain. Maybe they're seeking the best deal for tyres for their SUV. Or maybe they're simply trying to find a good site to help them raise their disgruntled teenagers better.

Whatever their problem is, relate to it. Your site must demonstrate in unequivocal and repeated terms that they are at the right place and that you have the answers. Demonstrate a clear and genuine understanding of their wants and needs–and they'll be far more willing to buy from you.

People need to see a headline or image that will draw them in and make them want to know more. It may be a tease: "Click here for a FREE e-Book that solves all your problems". Or it could simply offer a detailed description of how your services, if purchased, will solve their problems or bring them the solution they need to prosper in their business.

Design costs

Naturally, you will be paying more for a custom-designed website than for a template solution. The costs of a custom design vary enormously as some high end graphic designers may charge thousands of dollars for designs. However for a small business there are many talented designers out there who can provide quality design for a much lower amount.

Choosing a Web Designer / Developer

This is the $64,000 question. How do you choose a good one? Well, the usual rules apply. Research them, ask around, and get recommendations. Design particularly is a fickle area – I have worked with many talented designers whose designs I have hated. In many cases it is about style.

Here are some tips:

- **Take a look at the portfolio** – Do you like their work? Are you representative of your client base? If not, find people who are and get them to take a look.
- **Talk to them** – How easy will they be to work with? How open are they to your ideas? One arrogant designer once told me that if a client did not like her work it was simply that they did not understand it. A good designer should provide advice and direction, but still take on board your desires.
- **Talk to their clients** – Give a call to the companies that the designer has worked for. They may have a nice site, but how was the process? Long and arduous? Painless and exciting?

The Cool Factor...

Beware of the cool factor when dealing with a web service supplier. There are two broad skills required to create a website: design and development and they are very, very different. To simplify it, designers are artists and developers are geeks.

If you talk to some designers, they will focus on beautiful design, colours, look and feel and what they deem to be cool. If you talk to a developer they will create whiz bang things that flash and do cool stuff. Neither of these is in its entirety what you need and neither of these people will have asked you what the business reason is for this website.

So, beware of the one man band. I am not saying that it is impossible for a good designer to be a good developer and also be able to focus on your business goals – but it is rare. A good site needs to be built by a team. Designers, developers, content editors, and SEO/SEM specialists. If you are looking for someone to build your site, you are probably safer going with a reputable company rather than an individual.

It's All About the Words

I had a client at one time who was happy to spend thousands on his website. We spent a lot of time working on design elements, and the latest technology to make the site graphically interesting and fully functional. When it came to content, we asked him how he wanted to proceed and his response was that they had a work experience girl at the office and that she had time to write the content. In one fell swoop, he destroyed any chance for this site to reach its potential.

People often forget the content – they get carried away with the look and feel or the bells and whistles. Content is king. No matter how good the site looks, if the information is not well written, informative and compelling, the site will not be effective.

While most business owners will be able to jot down notes for what they want, it is nevertheless beyond their normal competency to write professional copy, because:

- Most people aren't great writers
- Most people don't see the value in writing and sharing expertise
- Most people don't believe they have time to write.

For this reason we encourage the use of content authors or editors. There are many professional writers out there and the majority are not too expensive. There are two ways to approach this aspect of your website.

1. **Content Authors** – These people will come to your office and pick up all your current marketing material, conduct interviews with you and your key staff and then write from scratch the content of your site. This is time consuming (and therefore more costly) but should provide a pretty good outcome.
2. **Content Editors** – In this case, you work with your content editor to define a structure and then you write the initial draft. You have the information required in your head, so just dump it all on paper and then give it to the editor to make it work. I believe that this is ultimately the best solution as well as a less expensive one.

The investment in a copywriter does not have to be massive. Search for copy or content writer and you will

find many providers (e.g. www.RainmakerMedia.com.
au) who will charge from $50 to $5,000 (depending
on number of pages) to write your website copy. You
need to be very clear in what you want. You will need
to specify whether you want search engine relevant
content or whether you will be using the website as a
marketing tool (as in email marketing).

No matter which option you prefer, look seriously
at content writers.

How to choose a copywriter or writing service?

I think the best way is by reading their work. Look
for a style that suits the feeling you want from the
site (corporate, friendly, humorous...). Ultimately
you are looking for something that will resonate with
your clients – and you know your clients better than
anyone.

Content Management Systems

Content management systems (CMS) essentially give
you administrator access to your website so that you
can modify the content on the site. By content I mean
the words and some of the images. These days, most
quality websites will have their own CMS. Years ago,
however, you'd pay quite a lot of money to have somebody build you a website, then, two weeks down the

track, you'd be thinking, "Mmm, I'd really like to change some of those words in that first paragraph."

A that point you would have to go back to your web developer who would charge you even more money to make those changes. These days, a CMS is essentially a back end to your website that you can log into. And by using an editor that probably looks a bit like Microsoft Word you can change the content on your own website.

So you can change all the words yourself. You can upload photos and images and move things around, and even change your menu structure. A CMS gives you quite a lot of control over your website.

These days you can get very cheap websites that may not have that, but most quality systems, even at the low end of the market, should provide you with a content management system.

Websites - Key Points

One stand-out point is that the website is a business tool and that a business tool needs to pay for itself in the same way that you intend an ad in the newspaper to give back *at least* as much as you spent on it.

You need to invest in your business tool, but you need to make sure you're getting that investment returned – typically, multiple times.

A mistake a lot of people make is to get too excited about owning a website without really having thought about why they need a website. Thus, they don't put a lot of thought into the content or the look and then they leave it; they don't update it, which means they don't get a return on their investment. Typically, the website doesn't act as a good representation of their business.

> What you need to do is treat the website like you would any investment. You need to measure its return on investment and track its effectiveness.

Now I've Got It, What Do I Do It?

Many people are confused about this because they believe that once they have their website then that's it, the job's done, they'll go to bed and wake up with money pouring into their bank accounts.

There are four things you need to do once you have your website:

1. You need to market it.
2. You need to manage it.
3. You need to measure it.
4. You need to optimise it.

Market It

Often when I tell people they need to market their website, they become confused because, as someone once said to me, they thought the website *was* the marketing. They therefore ask: why are we marketing something that does marketing?

The answer is of course simple. On the web, there are more websites than you can possibly count. For example, when you do a Google search, you'll often have millions of search results (some huge number). So the first thing you need to do is let people know about your website and if you have a website you're proud of, this should be relatively easy.

A couple of key suggestions: Make sure you have your website address at the bottom of your email signature; on your business cards, obviously; on your letterhead; on your window or door, if you have a shopfront; on any posters; on print marketing material; on anything that's public facing. If you send out any e-marketing, email newsletters, make sure there are a lot of links back to your website.

If you have suppliers or clients who are happy with you, ask them if they will link back to your website from their website. This does two things: one is that it provides some credibility and it gives people yet another way of finding you; and the second thing is that it's good for search engine optimisation. In fact, many search engine marketing experts suggest that this is one of the more important tactics for improving a website ranking as Google pays particular attention to these links and where they come from: the more popular a link is the more weighting Google will give to your website through these back links.

Manage It

I've seen plenty of people spend a lot of money on a website and once it's up and running, they get too busy to think about it again. It becomes a waste of money if you're going to do that. Your website needs to be maintained and kept fresh. Some of the ways you can do this are to create articles that you put on your website, and blogs (see later section), which are a type of article, or news items.

People need to have a reason to come back to your website. One of the best ways to market yourself in any business is to become an expert in your industry. And typically you are. For example, if you sell shoes, you know all about shoes, or if you're a mechanic, you know all about fixing cars. Become an expert and provide people with information.

If you can put on your website articles and pieces of information that enable people to learn something free of charge then they will be likely to come back. More importantly, not only will they come back, but when they're talking to one of their friends and the conversation leans toward that area, they will be likely to direct that person to your website.

At some stage, some of those people are going to be in a position to be buyers of your service or your product. And where are they going to go? They're going to go to the expert. Thus positioning yourself as an expert can pay dividends. And this is a general marketing tip for even more than just web technology because it's something you can do outside of the web. In short, the web is an excellent place to advertise and push your own credibility.

News on your website

It often seems unlikely to many website owners that they should post news items on their website. The point is that if people are to come to your website they are more likely to come back if you make an effort to keep up-to-date with your news items. One of the worst things you can do is having the latest news on your web page that is a year or two years old. This shows you're not interested in your website and gives others an indication of how you run your business – which is hopefully a false one, but customers don't know that from looking at the site.

So if news items are updated every month or so, that's a good indication of whether you're on top of your business.

If you have an e-commerce store, change it around a bit: move products around, add new categories, and change things that are on special because if people see different items on special every time they go to your website they will keep coming back. Particularly for e-commerce, you need to get people coming back to your website, so use weekly specials to attract buyers. In fact some businesses are built on that principle alone. Consider the case of this fantastic business model which has really extended the principal of promoting not just weekly specials but daily specials on the website.

JumpOnIt (www.jumponit.com.au) is an illustration of a global trend of collective buying companies which use technology and social media to change the way consumers buy. The business offers a special each day to its database of members who are given the opportunity to buy a service or a product at a heavily discounted price. Sales director James Gilbert says buying as a collective offers benefits all round. "We provide inner city people with brilliant deals, the best things to do, eat and buy in their city. We target inner city dwellers and businesses within the zone."

He says "Our demographic is people living near the inner city in 20-40 age group. It's your urban types; people in their 20s to 40s, who have disposable income, are going to restaurants, the theatre. These people will have done those things anyway, so it's good for them. For the business owners it's free exposure to significant new customers at no upfront costs.

"We promise the featured business that they will get a certain number of sales. They tell us how many people need to buy before it is worth their while to offer a special discount. Until we reach that magic number the deal is pending. When enough people sign up for it the deal is live.

"When that magic minimum number kicks over, the person will receive an email notification and a coupon that gets redeemed at the business. For example, we sold 5000 Hoyts tickets in one day and 500 massage sessions at Sheraton on the Park."

He says the benefits are significant for their members and participating business. "Say a restaurant offers a voucher with a value of $100. We sell this for say $50. For each 100 coupons sold the business receives $2500 plus pre-paid customers. We might receive $2500. For the business, it's picking up customers who may become repeat customers. They're investing only in people who come through the doors."

Jump On It is an illustration (a very spectacular one at that) of harnessing this notion of offering your dedicated website visitors something special. This method harnesses the power of bulk buying to save consumers money, and creates a win-win for the featured businesses. Gilbert says one of the keys to their success has been the fact that the partners in the venture have an accumulated 35 years experience in the digital space with a very large Facebook fan base. The businesses become profitable by taking a cut from each business that offers goods or services on the site. The operators of the sites claim that the online presence offers the ability to reach a target market faster.

Measure It

This relates back to what I was saying about your website being a business tool that needs to pay for itself. If it's not paying for itself, you must change something: either don't do it or make it work. And you can't know if it's paying for itself if you can't measure it. You can't manage anything if you don't have the information.

The most effective way to measure your website's success is the Google Analytics tool, which is a generation ahead of most products out there and it's free. You can set up Google Analytics on your website; it's very easy to do but you may need a web developer to help you with it which shouldn't cost much at all and then you can track *everything* going on with your website.

This system is good in that you can find out the number of visitors to your site, the people who've visited more than once and how many times and where they come from. It's interesting to find out how long they've stayed on your website and then track that over time. For example, if you have a lot of good articles people might be staying longer to read them.

Tracking your CTAs (call to actions) and your clicks, how many times a certain link is clicked, which products are the most popular, which pages are the most popular. You can even track how people flow through your website, for example, as in when people hit the home page, 73 per cent of them go to the About Us page next, or 37 per cent go straight to the online store and once they're there, 57 per cent of those people go to Category X first.

That's very important information. Another important factor is that you can find out where people are visiting your site from. For instance, you can find out geographically where they're coming from which is interesting if you're selling internationally. More importantly, you can find out whether they're coming to your site from a search engine or from a link on someone else's website or if they're typing in your address directly.

Dashboard   Nov 29, 2010 - Dec 29, 2010

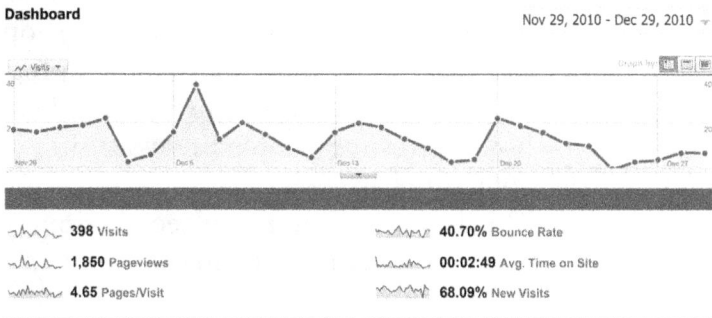

398 Visits		**40.70%** Bounce Rate	
1,850 Pageviews		**00:02:49** Avg. Time on Site	
4.65 Pages/Visit		**68.09%** New Visits	

This first section is showing us that in the period from 29th November 2010 to 29th December 2010, this site has had:

- 398 visits – that's 398 people coming to the website
- 1850 page views and 4.65 pages per visit.

- o Each time you click on a link or menu item in a page, you are opening a new page – which is called a page view. So, in the above example, on average people are clicking on 4.65 links in the site.
- 40.70% bounce rate
  - o A bounce is when someone arrives and then leaves from the same page on your site without surfing to other pages. A bounce rate of 30% is about average – I have rarely seen sites with much less than that. A bounce rate of 40% and above means that something is wrong and should be looked at.
- Average time on the site is 2 mins and 49 seconds.
  - o Internet wide, it is considered that a website gets about 45 seconds of someone's attention before they go elsewhere. While it is highly dependent on the type of site and the demographic, this is a useful metric to use as a guide to how interesting people find your site.
- 68.09% of visitors are new
  - o This is a good metric to see how many people return to your site a second and third time.

There are 4 sections in this page. Moving clockwise from top left:

- This is a graph showing visits over the month.

- o This is an excellent tool to track internet and non-internet marketing campaign results.
- Geographic spread of visitors
  - o Depending on your target market, this is quite useful to see where your website readers are coming from.
- Content Overview shows which pages of your website are the most highly viewed.
  - o This gives a good understanding of what interests the readers – and so you can focus more on that.
- Traffic Source shows how people are finding your site. There are 3 ways:
  - o Direct – these people are typing the web address into the browser. Meaning they know about you already (perhaps from business cards, word of mouth and traditional marketing methods)
  - o Referrers – these are other websites that link back to your site. This is a great way to track the effectiveness of your web partnerships.
  - o Search Engines – these are where people have found you via a search engine (like Google).

Each of these items above can be clicked on to go into more detail.

Because your website is one of your main marketing and sales tools you can also use Google Analytics to track non Internet-based marketing. So imagine a scenario whereby you've put an ad in two different newspapers, giving slightly different website addresses for

Twitter Me Dead!

Visitors Overview

30
15
30
15

310 Visitors

view report

Map Overlay

view report

Traffic Sources Overview

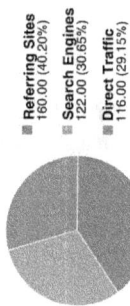

- **Referring Sites** 160.00 (40.20%)
- **Search Engines** 122.00 (30.65%)
- **Direct Traffic** 116.00 (29.15%)

view report

Content Overview

Pages	Pageviews	% Pageviews
/	340	18.38%
/home.php	195	10.54%
/contact.php	112	6.05%
/webservices.php	59	3.19%
/portfolio.php	50	2.70%

view report

each ad (e.g. two different pages on your site). You can then track how many people clicked on each of those different links so you can see the return on each newspaper ad investment. In the language of marketing, this is known as split testing and is a feature of the power and flexibility of internet marketing and its effectiveness in terms of tracking and adjusting to results.

From there, if you're selling something online you can track how many people go from the ad and buy products. Then you have a financial return on investment for your newspaper ad. If you have a brochure-style website, you can track how many people are going through to the Contact page, entering information in the Contact form or perhaps ringing you up. Obviously, you can't track the calls very easily, but you can find out how many people get to your Contact page.

Optimise It

Optimising your website is essentially, trying to get it found on the Internet. The analogy I use is: imagine someone has rented a shop location in an expensive street in Sydney, spends thousands of dollars renovating that shop, putting up attractive signage, laying out the store with quality floorboards and then covers up the front window and all the signage with brown paper and sits back and waits. They wait and wait to see if anybody comes into their shop. No-one comes into their shop because they don't know it's there.

The same applies for a website. If you just put your website online, then it's one of a hundred billion websites on the Internet and probably no-one will find it. There are two ways to get it found - I've mentioned the general marketing method – used within your local physical world that will push people to your website.

But how do you get your website found on the Internet by people you don't come into contact with who are not within your local environment? There are three answers: search engine optimisation (SEO) and search engine marketing (SEM) and other inbound links (like social media). To explain the difference between the first two, the analogy I use is that *SEO is a cruise ship: it can take you a long way, but it's slow to get started and it's very difficult to turn. SEM is a speedboat; you can turn it on or off very quickly, you can change both speed and direction very quickly.*

> SEO is a cruise ship: it can take you a long way, but it's slow to get started and it's very difficult to turn. SEM is a speedboat; you can turn it on or off very quickly, you can change both speed and direction very quickly.

SEO and SEM need to work together, hand in hand.

Search engine optimisation (SEO)

Do I need SEO for my website? It depends. SEO is used by business owners who want to get prospects through their website and convert them into new clients. If you are looking to build your business, SEO is a great resource that will only become more and more relevant in the future.

The operative word in SEO is optimization. SEO is an effort to optimize your website to attract traffic from search engines.

The algorithms rank your site based on how frequently your keywords are repeated in your site's copy as well as many other methods.

When you look at a Google page, after you've typed in a search, you will see on down the centre of the page what's called the 'organic search results'. Organic search results are Google's way of saying how relevant a website is compared with the search term you've keyed in. For Google, it's all about relevance. Google determines relevance by searching millions of sites and cataloguing the results, then returning the most closely related sites. They do this by using bots (robots or crawlers) that run around the Internet hitting websites. When they get to a website they look at a few different things.

They look at the keywords behind your website and they look at the content on your website to gather a picture of your site, and they grab some of those words and they look around your website and they'll give you a score, a ranking. Then they'll find any links on your website and follow those away from your site and hopefully with time, they'll find another website that links back to you. Knowing they've been on your site before, they look at you again and at where they've come from, and they 'think', "OK, I've come from this particular site which is all about selling shoes and your site says you're selling shoes, therefore, in regard to shoe sales, you must be valid."

You've gained relevance, so they add a few more points for this. There are whole heap of things that will add or remove SEO points. Ultimately, when somebody types 'shoes' into Google's browser it will look in its database at the various rankings and pull up websites in order of ranking.

To see the keywords on your site, look for the 'name="keywords"' line in your web page source file. To see this file, simply right-click with your mouse on the background of your home page and select 'view source'.

Websites

accountant wollongong | **Search**

Advanced search

Instant is on ▼

About 155,000 results (0.16 seconds)

Organic Search Results (SEO)

Wollongong Accountants
Wollongong Accountants... AccountantList.com.au - Helping you find an **Accountant** in Australia...26 Ralph Black Drive **Wollongong** North. NSW 2500 ...
www.accountantlist.com.au/x1611-Wollongong-Accountants.aspx - Cached

Accountant Wollongong ☆
Accountant Wollongong... Pay less tax, make more money and secure your financial future - Ask about our 2 for 1 tax return special offer.
accountantwollongong.com/ - Cached

Accountants Wollongong - Wollongong Accountants & Tax Agents... ☆
Accountants Wollongong... **Wollongong Accountants** & Tax Agents. 2 for 1 Tax Return Special Offer - Who Else Wants To Pay Less Tax, Increase Business Profits...
www.accountant-wollongong.website.com.au/ - Cached - Similar

Ⓐ 336 Keira Street, Wollongong
☎ (02) 4223 3152

Beedles & Wiseman - Accounting & Taxation Services... ☆
Beedles & Wiseman **Accountanting** is a CPA practice situated in **Wollongong**. We provide **Accounting** and Taxations services to Individuals, Small Businesses and....
www.bewise.com.au/ - Cached - Similar

Ⓑ 32 Market Street, Wollongong
☎ (02) 4225 0816

Russo & Co. Accounting ☆
We are a **Wollongong** based **Accounting** firm established in 1998, specialising in accounting, taxation and compliance services....
russoandco.com/ - Cached

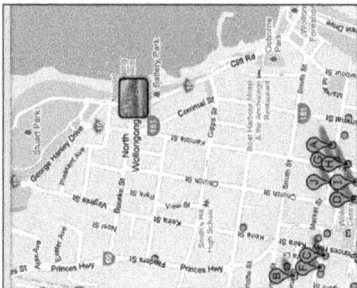

Place page

Place page

Twitter Me Dead!

```
<!DOCTYPE html PUBLIC "-//W3C//DTD XHTML 1.0 Transitional//EN" "http://www.w3.org/TR/xhtml1/DTD/xhtml1-transitional.dtd">
<html xmlns = "http://www.w3.org/1999/xhtml" >
<html>
<title> Web Design >> Graphic Design >> Web Development >> Wollongong Web Designer >> SEO >> Web Development >> Wollongon, Australia || Yuranga Web Des
<meta http-equiv = "content-type" content = "application/xhtml+xml; charset=UTF-8" />
<meta name = "description" content = "Web Design Company specialising in Web Design, Print Design, Graphic Design, Web Development, Web Hosting, Sea
<meta name = "keywords" content = "Web Design, Web. Design, Website Development, Wollongong, Illawarra, Australia, Web design Wollongong. Graphic Des
<meta name = "author" content = "Yuranga Web Design and Web Development, http://www.yuranga.com" />
<meta name = "verify-v1" content = "xa8lJVb720QOin2d/ zVvDmA0wCPab/ exQSWQ9yz2t5M=" />
```

So how do you get more points to increase your ranking?

1. **Content**: If you are selling shoes, you need to talk about shoes in your content. Often, the uninitiated will publish content something like this: "I'm John and this is my business, which my wife Mary and I started 25 years ago. We focus on customer service and blah blahblah…"
There are two problems with that. One is that it's boring and, two; it's not relevant for search engines. If you have an insurance consulting service then those are the words you need to see: 'insurance' 'investment'. If you're only servicing a local area, then you need to include words relevant to that, such as "red shoes Wollongong", which is relevant for anyone searching 'red shoes Wollongong'. In marketing, both online and offline, you should be speaking in terms of benefits to the customer and not in terms of personal biographies (that can come in at another less relevant part of the website).

2. **Keywords**: You can't always see (meta) keywords. They sit behind the website and they're your way of telling Google 'this is what we're all about. We're all about red shoes in Wollongong.' In the past, people thought search engine optimisation was all about keywords, which is now not true. Today, content is by far the most important because ultimately Google is trying to answer the question of relevance.

3. **Understanding who your competitors are:** When I
    ask people who their online competitors are, they
    usually list a few companies that are local com-
    petitors and who have websites. This is a common
    error. Often, your online competitor is not even
    selling the same items as you – they are not busi-
    ness competitors, but provide competition for po-
    sition in search results for certain keywords. Let's
    look at the local cane outdoor furniture retailer.
    Your online competitors are the sites that appear
    when someone searches 'cane furniture' or 'cane
    outdoor furniture' or 'cane furniture Sydney'.
    In some cases these results may not even be sites
    selling the same goods as you. There may be the
    'cane furniture appreciation society' or the 'cane
    furniture importers group' or 'how to make your
    own cane furniture' websites. While these organi-
    sations are not trying to compete with you on a
    business level, they may be the top ranked sites
    in the search engines for those keywords and as
    such are your competitors.

4. **Realise that Google does not understand imag-
    es:** While an image rich site looks good it is not
    very helpful to the search engines. Make sure
    you have lots of text with your images and use
    the *alt* tag behind your images (you may need
    to check with your developer on this one).

5. **Use relevant page titles:** See at the top of your
    web browser the title of the page you are view-
    ing? Often this is just left blank or as the name
    of your site. This should change for each page
    and be full of keywords.

There are a lot of tricks and techniques to improve SEO, but the bottom line is that SEO isn't something you can't do easily yourself. You need to have professional support. You need to understand who your competitors are on the Internet and work out ways of beating them by gaining more points.

That's the cruise-ship approach. The reason that it's so slow is that it takes time; it can take up to three months for your initial search engine results to take effect. So whenever you make a change that takes more time because Google has to re-evaluate it and give you more points. It's important to have an SEO strategy from the start, think about it and get it right and get it going for the long-term.

Search Engine Marketing (Pay Per Click)

SEM (also known as Pay Per Click or PPC) is different because it's for burst marketing campaigns. It centres on paid search traffic rather than the more organic, free search we have been describing to this point. Thus if you sell products online, you might choose to do an SEM campaign around Father's day –you set up a campaign (entering images and very short content) that will turn up in the right-hand Google search results page as a paid advertisement. Turn on a campaign a few weeks before Father's Day and start to see a big rise in traffic to your site.

Twitter Me Dead!

About 155,000 results (0.16 seconds)   *Organic Search Results (SEO)*

Wollongong Accountants
Wollongong Accountants... AccountantList.com.au - Helping you find an **Accountant** in
Australia...26 Ralph Black Drive **Wollongong** North. NSW 2500 ...
www.accountantlist.com.au/x1611-Wollongong-Accountants.aspx ... Cached

Accountant Wollongong ☆
Accountant Wollongong... Pay less tax, make more money and secure your financial future -
Ask about our 2 for 1 tax return special offer.
accountantwollongong.com/ - Cached

Accountants Wollongong - Wollongong Accountants & Tax Agents... ☆
Accountants Wollongong... Wollongong Accountants & Tax Agents. 2 for 1 Tax Return Special
Offer - Who Else Wants To Pay Less Tax, Increase Business Profits...
www.accountant-wollongong.websyte.com.au/ - Cached - Similar

(A) 336 Keira Street, Wollongong
(☎) (02) 4223 3152

Beedles & Wiseman - Accounting & Taxation Services... ☆
Beedles & Wiseman **Account**anting is a CPA practice situated in **Wollongong**. We provide
Accounting and Taxations services to Individuals, Small Businesses and...
www.bewise.com.au/ - Cached - Similar

(B) 32 Market Street, Wollongong
(☎) (02) 4225 0816

Russo & Co. Accounting ☆
We are a **Wollongong** based **Accounting** firm established in 1998, specialising in
accounting, taxation and compliance services...
russoandco.com/ - Cached

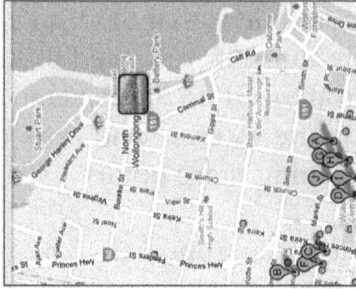

Place page

Place page

SEM can be quite complex, but essentially you're bidding for your position. Thus, if you have bid a higher amount than others vying for the same keywords, you're in a higher position. You pay each time somebody clicks on your ad. Therefore, if nobody clicks on your ad, you don't pay. If you're in a very competitive market, you may have to pay $15 or $20 per click or you may only have to pay 5 cents per click.

If the site in first place is currently paying 15 cents per click and you bid to pay 20 cents per click that will then put you above them into first position. Be aware that people are 40 per cent less likely to click on the advertising on the right-hand side than on the organic results because people realise that the organic results are all about relevance and the right-hand side is in fact advertising.

Nonetheless, regular and well-positioned SEM or Google Adwords Campaigns are very important and can do wonders for your business.

Although I use Google and Google Adwords as the discussion point here, there are other search engines, such as Yahoo! and Bing, and each of them has their own paid advertising components. One of the main reasons I talk about Google is because in the Australian search engine market, Google controls 74 per cent of the users. In the United States, Yahoo! is much stronger and competes well with Google.

Finding a niche.

People are often reluctant to do work within a niche because they want to be everything to everybody. One of the problems with this is that you're competing with everyone else who's doing *any* of the same things. For example, if you sell shoes, focusing only on selling shoes is going to be difficult because you're competing against everybody else in the world who sells shoes online – including large conglomerate shoe retailers with giant marketing budgets.

If you choose to compete for keywords in this broad space, you may end up on page 450 on Google, and that's not going to help you. If you're not on page one, perhaps at the top of page two, it's not going to be worth it. It's better to focus for only 5 per cent of the search results but appear on page one.

For example, that might be geographic localisation. If you're selling in a certain area – Sydney, Wollongong, for example – then focus on that and don't worry about the people selling in other states or the US. If you think there's a niche market for a particular type of shoe – wooden clogs or bright-red shiny shoes – focus on those keywords which will bring you a much better result for that small subset of the market than having a generic term.

This is a standard marketing strategy and it applies more so on the web because your competition is so much larger. In practice, what the contemporary, online business owner does is select a niche and use specific, niche terms to describe their product or service, for example "ballet shoes Sydney".

Increasing traffic to your website is one of the best ways to expose your business to new customers, create new sales, and boost your company's revenue. When used alongside SEO, pay per click advertising is an excellent way to create a well-rounded marketing strategy. Pay per click marketing is an ever-growing method of improving your company's online presence. Due to its relatively high ROI and targeted advertising capabilities, PPC is fast gaining ground as a legitimate player in the marketing world. Not only does PPC have the potential to be low-cost, high-efficiency, pay per click marketing is inherently trackable, since its aim is drive people to your website.

Setting Up a PPC Campaign

Before we begin talking about how to get more traffic on AdWords, we need to understand the concept of QUALITY traffic. We know not all traffic is created equal. I'd rather get 10 targeted visitors who want exactly what I have to offer rather than a thousand untargeted visitors who will take no action.

Keywords

It all starts with keywords. Coming up with keywords is often a time-consuming project and can be very frustrating. Google actually has a keyword tool that can help. It works like this. Google, with the development of their AdWords program, has put out a tool for all of us in the website business. It's called the Adwords Keyword Tool (https://adwords.google.com/select/KeywordToolExternal) and it, just like all things Google, is extremely user friendly. When you find yourself at the Keyword Tool homepage, you have to choose one of two options: enter your text, or type in your URL and let Google search your website.

The first option allows you to type in a word or a few phrases. Google then returns upwards of 100 other keywords related to yours. Also, Google gives you a rough estimate of how many searches for that particular word occurred last month, an average occurrence and the amount of advertiser competition for a listed search word. Typing in "Plumber Sydney", for example, returned pages of sites which were only referral sites. Some of the suggestions were "Emergency Plumber, Bondi", "Blocked Drains, Bondi".

Once you have your results, you can use the suggested words to narrow down the most effective words based on their number of searches for that particular term and the competition from advertisers. Keep in mind, keywords and phrases need to be from the viewpoint of the person who will be searching for your site. For example, if you are looking for a dentist, you would not type in dentistry, but rather dentist.

Make sure to take that into consideration when choosing from the generated search terms. Then, you can weave these words and phrases into your website content, articles, blogs and more. Google AdWords Keyword Tool is a free tool that has the potential to be very profitable. It is simple to use, but extremely effective and can help you find the keywords that your consumer will be searching and ultimately draw more traffic to your website.

Mistakes that waste time and money

The first mistake is to have a list of less targeted keywords. PPC campaigns depend on the keyword list on which you bid on to get your adverts displayed. Visitors then click on these ads and are directed to your website where you can engage them in a sales process. So a keyword list is literally your means of prospecting for customers. For example, if you target the term 'taxes' for your financial or investment business, you'll likely get poor results.

Another mistake is the failure to identify a unique aspect of your product or service (Unique Selling Proposition). All tax returns are essentially the same. They lead to paying taxes. Yet there is that thing that makes each uniquely different. Does your tax prep lead to tax savings? Do you always get returns filed on time? Always present the unique side of your product or service because that is what sells. It makes your advert to stand out of the crowd and gives a surfer reason enough to click it.

Mistake number three is the use of a broad match only. In keyword matching, you have four settings. This allows you to target your visitors with more specificity. The broad match option allows a multiple word keyword to show for any query with the terms, no matter the sequence of the words. For example, if you bid for the term 'free consultation' using broad match, your advert will also show when a surfer searches for 'consultations free'.

The fourth mistake is using only one adgroup. Keywords in an adgroup share an advertisement. Google AdWords allows you to have as many adgroups as you need. It is best to group very closely related keywords in one adgroup. For instance, separate keywords that are related to 'taxes' from those related to 'financial services' even though they all lead to the same product page. This helps in keeping bidding prices lower.

Ad writing

The first thing you need to understand about writing ad copy is that the copy must speak directly to the searcher. The major difference between PPC and traditional advertising is that you must communicate with your audience in as few as 95 characters; not words, but characters. In order to attract customers with your PPC ads, you need to say something good, and you need to say it quickly.

It's important to grasp the fact that behind every search term is a human being looking for something unique or of interest. Yet how am I going to write ONE ad that will be clicked on by people who want 100-200 different things? You can't do it. Your words will need to be as focused as possible. This means sticking only a handful of keywords in an ad group.

All the keywords will have basically the same theme. You can't get lazy on this, it's not good enough to say since notebook and laptop means the same thing we'll just write one ad for both keyword themes. It will cause your CTR (Click Through Rate) to go down and your cost per click to go up. If you write good ads and have good content on your website, Google will reward you. If you write an ad about tennis shoes and take them to a page on your website about tennis rackets, Google will penalize you. How?

Let's say you are advertising the shoes and have a website all about tennis shoes. I have a website about tennis rackets and a little about tennis shoes. Somebody types in a search that is 'tennis shoes' My ad appears and your ad appears over to the right of the organic search because we both have the keyword phrase 'tennis shoes' in our ad campaigns. I have bid a maximum of $3.00 per click and you have bid $1.50. Even though Google knows I have bid more they will place your ad above my ad or not even run my ad at all. So it is important. Also if I am up against someone else that has the same search term and I am $1.50 bid and they are $1.00 but my ad and landing page are the best, Google will only charge me $1.01 to be in the first position. When you win the first position, you are only charged 1 cent more than the next person's ad.

You should always be asking yourself what's going through the searcher's head! It is not easy and it requires some thought. You need to put yourself in the searcher's shoes and ask yourself what you would be thinking if you had this specific problem? What would be going through your head? What would be your biggest concern or fear? We then use this in the ad.

Adwords expert Ewan Watt offers few pointers. "We recommend that you utilise the Google Adwords Keyword tool to ascertain the total amount of local monthly search for each keyword per month. As a general rule, it is fair to conservatively estimate that your site will receive approximately 3% of the total search in the first 3 months and this may increase to 6-7% in the 3-6 months period. Obviously the results will vary dramatically, but this at least provides your business a guide as the amount you should invest in SEO.

"When calculating the potential return from search engine optimization you should work on a sales lead conversion rate of 3% and lead close rate of 20-25%. The lead close rate from search engine optimisation is generally higher than other forms of marketing due to the fact the person has already pre-qualified their interest by the keyword they typed into Google. If you are running an Adwords campaign the traffic forecast exercise for SEO is even easier."

Social Media

Everyone's talking about what to do with it. Social media, for marketers, is both a headache and a hot opportunity. Can it drive sales? Should it enhance customer relations? Is it a research tool? Does it lift brand awareness? Is it worth the time? The answer to all those questions is yes; but experts are all over the place on the question of how.

There are so many keywords and catchphrases going around that it's very difficult for a lot of small businesses to really understand the relevance to their business and whether they actually need to be involved in these things.

I'm sure you've all heard of Facebook, MySpace, LinkedIn, Twitter, blogs, social bookmarking, and crowdsourcing. They're all ways of using what we commonly refer to as Web 2.0 for communication. But the big question we really need to answer in this section of the book is whether these items are relevant to you. Can they add bottom line increases to your business?

Damon Fieldgate, executive general manager of Melbourne IT's SMB eBusiness Solutions division, positions social media as another communication channel. "While a lot of companies are still sitting on the fence when it comes to using social media, if you strip away the technology, at the simplest level social media such as Facebook and Twitter are just additional channels to communicate to your customers and prospects.

"Those 'followers and friends' that a business can attract through social media are a vital asset as they have chosen to actively engage with your company. The benefits for business are the ability to get real-time feedback, engage and build a rapport with customers that ultimately drives stronger sales."

Social media does appear to be where the action is, but will only trigger revenue where you have something so interesting that people want to use their own media to tell others about it. In the social media space, there is definitely a sense of camaraderie– people articulate the (presumably shared) experiences and values that identify themselves as belonging to a particular community. For business it's another form of engaging with consumers on their terms and gaining trust based on genuine understanding. Consumers don't trust advertising, but they do trust peer recommendation.

Research adds to the weight of evidence

According to Nielsen, nearly 20% of social consumers are now using social networks as their core navigation tool. Rather than utilizing search engines or content hubs such as Microsoft, Google, or Yahoo, these consumers are looking for content within social networks and clicking from there. In the early days of the Internet, new web content was discovered and promoted by editors at the major portals. Then search engines democratised the process, enabling each user to find what he or she was looking for. Now, social feeds—through which users follow what their friends (and friends of friends) are doing and recommending—are a primary path to web content.

Even Google and Bing (an up'n coming search engine) are recognising the trend by incorporating feed content from both Facebook and Twitter into search results and algorithms. Consumers are bombarded by messages, advertisements and the sheer volume of data available on the Web. With social networks now familiar tools, consumers are turning to their most trusted sources to help them sift through information. Trusting in the experiences and reviews of their friends or like-minded individuals, consumers are increasingly relying on social media for their major decisions, personal or commercial.

Before you can make any decisions about social media, the first thing you need to do is understand what they are. Hence I'm going to go through a few of them, in turn, to explain them.

Social Networking (Facebook / MySpace / Linked In)

First up, we can group together what we call the social networking sites (or software) – MySpace, Facebook and LinkedIn. MySpace started in 2003 and was the first real site of its kind to perform social networking. Social networking enables members of the site to contact each other, to communicate and interact with each other on the site.

MySpace was bought in 2005 by Rupert Murdoch for $580 million – so that's not a bad outcome in just a couple of years.

Facebook started in early 2004, and soon outpaced MySpace as the social networking site of choice. As at July 2010, Facebook had 500 million users, of which 50 per cent log in daily. That's a lot of people on one website.

Historically speaking, MySpace and Facebook were originally aimed at teenagers. It provided a place where kids could get online and just have fun, upload their music, talk about things and communicate with each other. However, with the popularity of Facebook, you'll now find people in their 30s are one of the largest demographics using Facebook. This is a really interesting fact if you want to start thinking about how to market to them.

LinkedIn started in May 2003. It's slightly different because it's effectively a professional version of Facebook and MySpace. Hence it's really for business because it's all about business networking. If you are interested in B2B-style networking, then LinkedIn is the place for you to be. See below for more information on Linked In.

Here are some statistics.

- MySpace has over 200 million users, split evenly between men and women 14 to 34 years old. Twenty-five percent of them are in the U.S.
- Facebook has over 510 million members, more women than men. The majority of these users – 80% – are under 30 years old and half of all Facebookers are located in the U.S., Great Britain and Canada.
- LinkedIn has over 80 million members, with the average age being 41. Men make up 64% of the audience. Their average household income is $109,000
- Twitter has an estimated 75 million users (more, depending on the source), two-thirds of whom are men 18 to 34 years old.

What to watch out for

One of the things you need to be careful about when you're looking at these sites is that they're primarily and originally – particularly MySpace and

Facebook – designed around non-commercial interaction. And one of the mistakes that a lot of people make early on is that they burn their credibility by trying to force commercial interaction through these sites. It's a big problem because what tends to happen is that people will create a Facebook page, invite people to be their friends and then start hammering them with commercial bits of information, which turns a lot of people off.

Therefore one of the things about the new media is that it's very good for communicating, but you need to be very careful what you communicate and how you communicate it. Somebody who is seen to be pushing commercial interaction may soon be tuned out or un-friended.

Facebook Fan Pages

One interesting part of Facebook is what is called a Fan Page. This is a page that is not tied to an individual person, but rather to an organisation or event or thing. A fan page allows people to become a fan and then be notified of updates. This is a very handy introduction of commercial concepts into an essentially non-commercial arena.

Simon Scholtens from Scholtens Real Estate (www.scholtensrealestate.com.au) uses fan pages to list his newest properties. Potential clients become fans and each time Simon updates his fan page with a new property they are notified by email with a link directly back to view the property. It's easy and immediate. It helps both the business and the client. It's a win-win.

Steps for Creating a Fan page

Creating a Facebook fan page is quite easy.

1. Login to your usual Facebook account or create one at www.facebook.com you need a regular account to create a fan page – and let's face it, you may as well, everyone else has one!
2. Go to http://www.facebook.com/pages/create.php
3. Decide what type of page you want. It's probably not a community page, but more likely a Local Business page, Company page or a Brand / Product page.

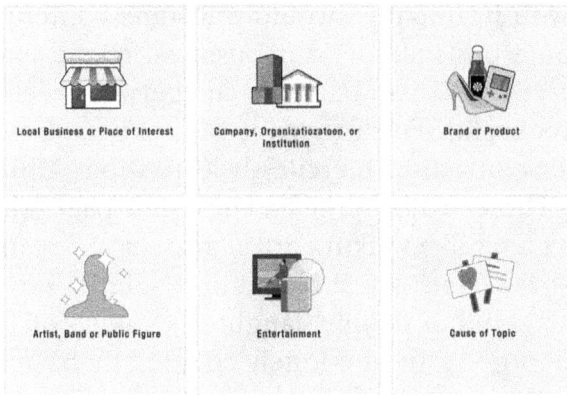

Local Business or Place of Interest	Company, Organizatiozatoon, or Institution	Brand or Product
Artist, Band or Public Figure	Entertainment	Cause of Topic

4. Enter the required details and click Get Started.

Company, Organization, or Institution
Join your supporters on Facebook.

| Choose a category ▼ |

| Company Name |

I agree to the Facebook Pages Terms

Get Started

Getting the page is easy. Now the question is what to do with it. Initially I would put some content in it. Add some posts about your business, recent exploits and successes. If you have any imagery or video, that is always useful. From there it is a matter of exploiting your contacts as mercilessly as possible. You need FANS! There is no point having a fan page with no fans. It's a bit like walking down a street of restaurants at 7:30pm. There are 2 restaurants side by side, one humming, full of people, laughter, clinking of glasses and the other with one lonely couple at a back table. Which do you choose? The one with the atmosphere right? It's the same thing here – you need to get a critical mass (the same applies for all the social media activities). Get some fans, get a few people to write some comments on your fan page and then publicise it to a wider network or clients and contacts.

LinkedIn

LinkedIn membership stands at over 80 million and like other social media sites like MySpace, LinkedIn has found its niche. Indeed it seems to have gone into a gallop in recent times. It took 477 days to reach the important milestone of 1 million members. The last million were added in just nine days.

Essentially, LinkedIn is a business-oriented website that provides a job exchange service. Most users are using the networking website as their digital résumé in order to attract job offers. In a business world where branding is a key element of survival, LinkedIn is a mecca for self-promotion. It has also signed up more than 60% of Fortune 100 companies for its hiring solution.

Its membership is also attractive from an advertising perspective–its average user is 41 years of age and has household income of more than US$105,000, making it one of the most affluent, large scale online audiences around.

The other social media tools do not have as much as of an agenda as LinkedIn. Users of the business-oriented network seem to spend more time professing what they know and don't spend as much time listening to others. This is the traditional media model of one-way communication, which is the style of communication that social media has displaced. For some, this seems like blatant self-promotion; for others it's better than going to endless (and expensive) lunches.

Whereas Facebook has become the social sharing network, Twitter is the thought-provoking, learning network, MySpace is the social relationship network, LinkedIn is the branding and résumé network. The demographics are settling in to reinforce the existing nature of each of the networks.

What is clear is that 2011 will be the year that social media marketing becomes more entrenched, followed by more competition by other networks seeking to improve or offer alternatives to the established services.

LinkedIn is not as powerful as a communication tool to contact potential candidates as some people don't want to be contacted through LinkedIn and it can feel like spam, but it is excellent for executive search research.

LinkedIn as a recruiting tool

Anecdotal stories abound around members recruiting other members through LinkedIn. The recruiting can be for executive jobs, consulting assignments or for business opportunities. There are people who devote time each and every day to form new connections and then, in turn, ensure that these connections get seen by other connections – a bit like matchmaking but more subtle. The opportunities are stark as it only takes a permission-based email to make contact with another member who can then take up discussions and indeed lead to employment, business and networking opportunities.

Reference checks

Entrepreneurs have to constantly make critical personnel decisions without sufficient information due to inadequate resources to quickly and effectively vet them.

LinkedIn helps find and reference check candidates and contractors by finding others they worked with for an unbiased, honest opinion.

You can use 'Service Providers' to quickly find those that have received recommendations from people in your network and other LinkedIn members. Past customer feedback is often more valuable than what a company or individual says in their marketing materials.

The Company information section is handy when compiling target company lists (see later) as well as finding out about the employment history profiles of people in client and target companies.

Market intelligence opportunity

Compared to larger enterprises, small businesses suffer from a dearth of relevant industry and competitive intelligence. LinkedIn enables you to follow a company if you need to:

- Be in the loop on key developments at the company
- See who has recently joined, left, or been promoted
- Stay informed of business opportunities, job openings, and more

Link "In" to Companies

Company Profiles are a powerful research tool that helps you find and explore potential companies to work for or do business with. Profiles feature a company overview, lists of people you know at the company, and unique data from the LinkedIn network.

Browse company profiles to view real-time information about the employees at relevant competitive companies or use Advanced Search to find ex-employees from relevant past companies that can provide balanced advice about the business model.

Accessing Profile

There are easy ways to access Company Profiles on LinkedIn, including clicking on the Companies' option which takes you to the Company Search page. Here, in addition to being able to search for companies you want to research, you can find out which companies are the most viewed, fastest growing, and most connected.

What's in a Company Profile

Company profiles begin with a brief overview and are followed by two primary components: information about relevant people at the company and aggregated statistics about employees.

Your profile

Once you populate your profile on LinkedIn, it is discoverable through the millions of searches on search engines and on LinkedIn. You are in complete control over what others see on your profile, so leverage this to showcase your skills and talents so the right people and opportunities find you.

Snapshot

Your snapshot features an overview of your name, location, current title, past positions, education, recommendations, and links to your websites. Think of it as your next-generation business card.

Public Profile

Not surprisingly the LinkedIn headings read like a bio – and that's what it is with, only with extra bells and whistles!

Your snapshot also includes a link to your 'Public Profile' – the profile that will be shown to users not signed-in to LinkedIn that are searching for you via search engines like Google.

Consultants

Build your business as a consultant, demonstrate your areas of expertise, and leverage your network to keep in touch and up to date with past and present clients and co-workers through updates, status reports, etc. One day they may be in position to hire you for a project. The benefits are to:

- Make it easy for potential clients to find you in the service provider directory by getting recommended

- Include your vanity URL in RFP responses, so potential clients can quickly and easily see common connections who can provide additional perspective
- Connect with relevant professionals you meet while travelling who you think could be important contacts in the future. Don't take the chance that you might lose their business card.

It can be difficult to find the right expert advice given that many projects are so far-reaching and complex.

Tap into the human capital within your firm, or within your network if you freelance, to quickly find experts/contractors when you need additional help through the online search facilities on LinkedIn.

Business branding

Company Pages – apart from giving others the opportunity to snoop into your business –will enable companies to build their brand through network-aware recommendations, giving members rich, credible insights into how any given product (or service) is perceived by their fellow professionals.

Product or service recommendations from one's professional peers are among the most trusted forms of conveying product information. They play a critical role in helping professionals cut through the clutter in making time-sensitive decisions about key purchases.

Making intelligent recommendations helps define your professional persona as an influencer and helps you build credibility with potential employers, partners and colleagues. Most importantly, it offers additional value to your network of connections who may be looking for your recommendation before they make their next purchase.

Twitter

Twitter came out of nowhere and quickly became hugely popular. Twitter is all about posting Tweets. A Tweet is a short message like an SMS or a text of 140 characters or less which you post to the Twitter website. People who choose to follow you will be notified of those messages the next time they log in.

Now when you think about it, it's really quite ludicrous – the whole concept of Tweeting via Twitter – and yet despite only starting in 2006, by early 2010, Twitter users were posting 50 million Tweets per day. That's an enormous number of messages being communicated each day.

The idea is that you create a Twitter account, then your friends, colleagues or other people who are interested in what you may have to say will follow you.

It's entirely up to them; you can't add them onto your Twitter account yourself.

Twitter users can choose to Tweet something as banal as when they go to bed or when they get up and other boring stuff such as when they're making a cup of tea or what they had for breakfast. There is a lot of rubbish out there but if you manage to find a good group of people to follow and if you have some valuable content you can add, a Twitter account can be hugely beneficial to you.

Twitter is an excellent way of setting yourself up to be an expert in your industry. If you start Tweeting about particular events, situations or information relevant to your specialist area, then people will start to follow you and more people will hear what you have to say. Online a journalist on Twitter might see what you tweet about and read your blog post (see below), then you'll become top-of-mind if they're looking for a source for commentary.

Once again, with Twitter you need to be very careful with how you use it. Twitter is not about telling everybody about every special you have and talking nonstop about all of your new products. Because people can choose to follow you, if they're bored or annoyed by your Tweets, they can choose not to follow you as well. Therefore it's important to get a following then become an expert and create a centre of influence. Then if you build up a reputation and some respect, you can start gently telling people about what you do, about the products you have to offer.

Here are a few things which Twitter can do pretty well:

- It's an amazing form of distribution for ideas, information and content; it's short but some of the best tweets are just links.
- It's where things happen first. Increasingly news happens on Twitter before news organisations publish anything.
- As a search engine, it rivals Google. Twitter harnesses the mass capability of human intelligence as distinct from machine intelligence. It's the power of millions working to find information that is new, valuable, relevant and entertaining.
- It's a formidable aggregation tool – if you are following the most interesting people they will in all likelihood bring you the most interesting information.
- It's a great reporting tool – many of the best reporters, journalists, and sales reps are now habitually using it
- It's a series of common conversations – or it can be. As well as reading what you've written and spreading the word, people can respond.
- It's more diverse than traditional media.
- It changes the tone of a sales blurb – a good conversation involves listening as well as talking.

- It's a level playing field – a recognised name may initially attract followers in reasonable numbers. But if they have nothing interesting to say they will talk in an empty room.
- It has a more real news value: the power of tens of thousands of people articulating those different choices can wash back into newsroom where editors will now take note.
- It has a long attention span because of followers of a particular keyword or issue or subject and you may well find it having an enduring conversation.
- It creates communities – or rather, communities form themselves around particular issues, a kind of grass roots movement one could say – around cultural, sporting, entertainment, shopping, etc.
- It changes notions of authority from "expert" opinions to so-called peer to peer authority. A 21-year old student is quite likely to be more drawn to opinions of and preferences of people who look and talk like her. Or a 31-year old bloke passionate about politics and the rock music of his youth.

The downside of Twitter also means that the full weight of the world's attention can fall on a single unsustainable piece of information.

Blogging

Something that's been around for a while, longer than social networking and Twitter, is blogging. As with a lot of these things, blogging came out of the average 16-year-old girl's need to express her every feeling to the entire world. Blogs started with young people creating a website and just writing about their life – whining about their teachers, talking about their love lives, etc. to the world at large.

Blogs are open to anybody as long as they know how to access the site. You can't block people from viewing it once you've put the information online.

After a while, corporate users decided to get on the bandwagon. They figured these blogs might be an interesting way to approach their consumers. Highly placed individuals in Microsoft or Sun Microsystems started creating blogs as a way to communicate potential ideas or to get a feel for how things were going with their customers.

Corporate benefits

Blogging became interesting for the business market for a number of reasons. First of all, in a large organisation it's a way for a CEO, CFO or COO to pass on communication to staff in a more informal way than office memos and things like that. So they could simply type how they were feeling, how they thought the company was doing and where things were going and ask for ideas and feedback from the staff.

In the same way, the organisation can do the same thing for their clients. In the past, a company would have expensive focus groups, pre-launches and launches of products and the relevant trials. Now, the CEO has a platform to express ideas in a very personable manner. They can write on their blog that they're having a good or bad day, or that they've just released a new product or, rather, that they have an idea for a new product, and then wait to see what happens.

Blogs can be very important tools for hearing negative and positive feedback. You may find, for instance, rafts of clients speaking out about your bad idea. In this way you can get fast feedback about what the customer base is thinking, a feature which is very helpful in saving the company future financial outlay. It's a great way to test various versions of a new product launch.

A blog is also a way for a CEO to create a personal relationship with the client. They may be earning millions a year, but nonetheless everyone can see that they're really just a regular person, writing a blog, and that may make the product more accessible.

Of course, with the improved Internet speeds and the ability to post videos, one of the next most popular methods of communication is video blogging. Again, the teenagers started this first, but it's becoming popular to place a video of yourself talking instead of just typing the blog for people to read.

How to blog

If you're interested in having your own blog, there are a couple of ways to do it. You can use a pre-created system, such as www.blogspot.com and www.blogger. com, whereby you quickly create an account, choose a template and start writing your blog.

Another way to do it is to get blogging software and install it on your own website such as www.word-press.com and www.moveabletype.com. There are two schools of thought about this, but my personal choice is that if you have a website you're trying to drive people to then it's a good idea to have your blog on that web-site as it maintains continuity. However, a lot of people argue that if you have it on something like BlogSpot, it's an easy way to direct people back to your website. Programs, including Drupal, Joomla and WordPress will typically allow users to build both a website and a blog. The benefit here is that you only have ONE login to access and update all of the content of your site. Plus, there's only ONE system to learn.

Step 1: Determine why you are blogging

Remember there are four reasons why a website exists to aid a business:

1) to build a brand
2) generate leads
3) generate direct sales or
4) generate advertising revenue.

A blog can also support any one of these goals. Which goals are you trying to accomplish with your company website and which are you trying to accomplish with your blog?

Step 2: Determine the concept of your blog.

What is the niche you will write about? Who will care? Once you know WHY you are blogging, you can think about WHAT to blog about. You may go back and forth between Step 1 and Step 2 for a few rounds before making your final decision. Some people start with an idea for a blog but when they put it to the revenue-generating test, the idea changes. Step 1 and Step 2 must work in tandem. You have to have an audience for what you have to say.

Your blog concept can be very narrow, attracting a small but passionate niche of readers and few, if any, competitors, or it can focus broadly on a topic that is widely popular but has a lot of competition. Much of your decision may rely on the resources available to you and ultimately your goals. Do you have a large marketing budget, staff and resources for your blog? Do you already have access to a large audience of readers (thousands to tens of thousands of readers)?

Do you have a long period of time (2-3 years) over which you can consistently devote 5-10 hours per week of writing and marketing efforts to slowly build your blog audience and subscriber base? If you answered no to all of these questions you may want to consider focusing narrowly since creating a very unique voice or speaking on a unique topic is a much easier and faster way to break through the noise than writing about the same thing that everyone else writes about.

Step 3: Will your blog be separate or integrated into your site?

Here you need to determine whether your blog will be under the same domain name as your site or not. The benefit of including it in the same domain is that you will get more SEO value out of the content of your blog. Some advise putting your blog under a different domain and linking generously between the two sites in order to gain link popularity. But link popularity is not necessarily the most important element of SEO (nor will it help you much to have many links between two sites, neither of which is itself highly ranked).

Having a larger base of keyword-rich content on your site is usually far more important. Having your blog hosted under the same domain name as your site will add all of your blog content to your site content when search engines determine where to place your site in the rankings. For more about search engine optimization read our section on pages....

You Tube

If you have any doubt about the role of YouTube in helping small businesses promote themselves, note that in 2008, when Google began including videos on its first page of search results, suddenly, online businesses everywhere had to not only think of optimizing text, but rich media as well. It should be noted that Google owns YouTube so that could also explain why a perusal of Google's search results will often include the same handful of businesses in the first page of search results.

There is certainly an important role for YouTube to play in the marketing of businesses seeking to get more visibility on line. Some researchers now believe users are more willing to click links they know lead to a video, no matter where the link is displayed. Also, eye-tracking studies have confirmed that users immediately gravitate toward video search results, often looking at a video thumbnail before the first link on the page.

Sharing videos over the Web is a great way for small businesses to establish a social media presence, particularly because of how many people are tuning in. According to a recent survey, Google's many video sites accounted for 12.2 billion videos viewed in one month earlier in 2010, including YouTube, which accounted for nearly 99% of the total.

YouTube: Statistics

YouTube started in 2005, then Google bought it in 2006 for US$1.65 billion. Currently, the most popular video on YouTube has had 185.39 million hits or views.

Uploaded To Date[6]:

- Over 5 billion videos
- 200,000 videos uploaded each day
- Last year 91 million viewers
- Every minute, ten hours of video is uploaded on YouTube
- Average time to watch:2 minutes 46 seconds
- Average age of the uploader: 26 years old

Look at these amazing statistics and ask yourself: "How can that work for my business?" It may not be for everybody, but once again it's a matter of thinking that there's a lot of stuff going on there and asking, "Can I be part of it and is it worthwhile?"

Think of Natalie Tran (www.natalietran.me) who reportedly earns a 6 figure income from advertising on her YouTube channel. Now, before you give up your day job, realise that only a very, very small percentage of content providers gain this sort of success.

One way to look at YouTube is as an advertising source and a way you can actually place ads on YouTube. The number of people advertising on YouTube has in-

---

6   Figures supplied by YouTube

creased tenfold in the past year. USA-based Advertising Age, reported that of the top 100 advertisers, 94 have run campaigns on YouTube.

The second way to make YouTube work for you is to use it to direct people to your website and to advertise your products and services. If you have a product or service that can be displayed or talked about in a video format then YouTube is the place to put it. By putting it on YouTube and linking it back to your website and posting some good keywords with it, people can find it, they can view it, they can click on it and then go back to your website.

This not only helps the individual make a potential sale but it helps with your search engine optimisation because it's a link back into your website (which Google gives value to). The next thing you can do is to embed your YouTube video into your website. So instead of people finding it on YouTube they can find it on your website. So people go to your website first, they see a YouTube video on your website, they click play and watch it then and there.

The thing that makes social media so interesting is that they can all connect together. For example, if you create a video on YouTube talking about your product or something related to it, you can then post a link to Twitter, and put the video on your website and then also post the video to Facebook. So from that one video source, you can use a few different social media arms to get your product or message out to people.

Thus by intertwining these arms, you get a multiplier effect as it's not just having one video on YouTube, it's having all your friends see it on Facebook and all your contacts on Twitter receiving information about it, as well as the people visiting your website. This can have the effect of adding traffic to your website.

Is it worth the trouble of creating a video?

- Go to http://www.YouTube.com and create your account.
- Write your bio in the first person tense (use "I") to make your profile more personal.
- Upload a clear and professional looking picture of yourself. It is vitally important that people understand that there is a real person in front of your business.
- Make sure to include as much personal information as possible including your favourite movies, books, TV shows, activities, etc.
- Include a link to your website at the TOP of your profile and at the bottom of your profile

In steps:

1. **Show how to use your product.** There are countless small business owners posting how-to videos on YouTube along the lines of "here's how to use the product" or "here's how to interact with people in our service industry."

2.   **Extend your client base**. Dr. Tony Eyers, a 51 year old IT trainer and harmonica player, has turned his passion for the harmonica into a business, pursuing a dream, in his words, "To play music with the best harmonica players in the world." Three years into setting up his business of selling harmonica lessons online, he has tapped a potentially rich vein of customers in China by posting videos on YouTube teaching people how to play harmonica. This has resulted in online revenue from visitors.

3.   **Entertain your customers**. It is quite easy to post a video simply for visitors' enjoyment. You could also add a tab such as a 'Videos we like' tab on your channel. For a small business owner, posting a video for entertainment purposes stands to generate many views, which in turn may spark interest in the company and possibly lead to the purchase of products or services.

Podcasting

Podcasting, like YouTube is about getting another type of media out into the marketplace. In this case, it is audio. Podcasts have become such a popular marketing tool for sole proprietors and small businesses that a small army of professional producers is out there waiting to help.

You need to:

1.   **Do some homework**. The best way to learn about podcasting is to listen to podcasts.

2.   **Decide on a topic**. Podcasts could focus on a company's products or services, an industry or on management or professional issues. Whatever the topic, make sure it's related to a company's business in some way.

3.   **Gather your tools**. Producing a podcast requires:
- A microphone, digital audio recorder or USB headset to record podcast episodes
- Computer with sound card and high-speed Internet connection
- Audio recording and editing software, either licensed software or free open-source programs such as Audacity.

4.   **Be natural**. When it's time to record a podcast, organize talking points, but don't use a script.

5.   **Build a backlog**. Before going live, build up a catalogue of a dozen or more episodes. Ideas can be sourced from talking to customers, going to conventions, reading trade magazines, or following current events.

6.   **Be consistent**. Length, professional quality, and subject matter of a company's podcast are important but not as much as on-air consistency. Whether it's once a day, once a week or once a month, pick a schedule and stick to it. Podcasts are like radio or TV shows: audiences expect a schedule.

7.   **Not a D-I-Y type**? Hire a pro. Professional producers can handle the technical aspects of starting or creating a podcast.

8.   **Forget about making money, at least not directly**. Podcasts should be part of a company's overall marketing strategy, to get yourself known, you have to blog,

optimize your website for search engines and podcast. If you do all three the results could phenomenal.

Crowdsourcing

Crowdsourcing is a new term. It's a Web 2.0 term that isn't actually a piece of software but it encompasses all the bits of software mentioned up until now – all the social networking and social media software.

Crowdsourcing is simply the ability to source information or skill sets or data from the world at large. Basically, it's putting a question out there and asking for an answer. It's something that you can do now very easily on the Internet if you have a lot of followers on Twitter or a blog, or you have lots of friends through MySpace, Facebook or LinkedIn.

Simply put the question out there: "I'm looking for a new employee. Does anybody know someone who might fit the bill?" or "We're thinking of doing this with our product line, what does everybody think?" or "Can somebody find me a web designer they'd recommend?" It can also include group effort on a project such as three designers joining forces to supply a new logo to a third party.

Thus instead of asking one or two friends, you're asking as many people as you have in your social network and then multiplying that by how many people they have in their network as well. Therefore you can reach a whole lot more people than you could individually and you can usually get the answer you're looking for.

Social Bookmarking

Has anyone heard of Digg (www.digg.com), which is one of the social bookmarking sites? Social bookmarking is the ability to have people mark your blog or your website or part of your website and have a link back to that information in another location, such as Digg. com. The idea is to make that public to other people. Thus, if you've written a particularly interesting blog post, people can click on an icon near your blog post, which will then put that into their Digg account and can then be made public for other people to see.

Therefore, it's a good idea to add functionality to your website and blog that allow people to be able to click on icon links such as www.digg.com and www.delicious.com and www.reddit.com.

Do I Need to Use Social Media?

To date I've covered some of the social networking and social media concepts. Now the questions we need to address that we posed in the opening paragraphs are, "What's the point? Do we really need to do this? Is this going to help me sell my product in my local area?" And the answer to that question is, "It depends".

It depends on how you use it. It depends on who your target market is. My belief is that you're not going to sell product on Facebook or LinkedIn or Twitter. You're not going to sell product on your blog or YouTube. You're going to sell product either in your store or on your website.

Some research conducted by the large internet services companies can help us understand some of the trends. Recent research by Melbourne IT found that those small businesses using social media were more likely to make higher revenues online than their non-social SMB brethren. In its research of 3,400 small businesses on how they use the Internet to do business, covering social media, mobile internet, cloud computing and more, around a third of SMBs polled used social media, with the favourite tools being Facebook and Twitter. The main reasons cited by those that didn't use social media were that they didn't see the business benefit or didn't have the time to manage it.

The aim of social media marketing is to build a whole heap of touch points around a core and that core will probably be your website or your business premises if you have one. Therefore, the idea is that you use these tools to put yourself out there in different locations on the Internet and drive people back to your point-of-sale – your website or your business premises.

A solid social media component has become a critical element of any marketing and advertising strategy, and is often used to complement other activities like print, TV, radio and online activities.

Twitter Me Dead!

Yesterday's stodgy newsletter has been replaced by today's interactive blogs and e-newsletters. Announcements by the old letterbox drop are now broadcast via Twitter. And word-of-mouth campaigns are now shared globally via Facebook. In truth, brands and businesses worldwide are embracing social media as a fresh and effective channel to communicate with customers, elicit feedback and improve the product.

According to a recent report by eMarketer, this year an astounding 60% of Internet users aged 35 to 44 – and one-half of those in the 45-to-54 age group – will use social networks at least once a month. The report also estimates that 57.5% of all Internet users will use a social network at least once a month in 2010. It goes on to predict that nearly two-thirds of all Internet users will be regular users of social networks in 2014.

Those numbers represent a significant shift from the current stereotype of a social network user as being primarily from the Generation Y segment. It seems that as more of the Gen X and Gen Y users begin using social networks, then their parents (i.e. Baby Boomers) will begin to log on as well – to view photos of their grandkids, share status updates and just keep in touch with members of their family.

As these people become accustomed (nay, addicted) to social media, they will be far more likely to seek out and/or trust the people, brands and businesses that are already in their social media community.

The bottom line here is that if you do not want to use social media, at least make it a conscious decision based on your own research. It does take time and effort, and often the results can take time to come to fruition. It's an investment, and you need to understand what you are investing in and what it will cost. If you choose to use social media as one of your marketing sources, then do it properly – plan it, and then execute it efficiently.

Measuring the Only Really Important Thing – Your Return on Effort

What is important is your return on investment (ROI). After all, the only real reason you're setting up, running and managing a social media campaign is to make money, right? As there are very few costs associated with social media campaigns, it's about return on *effort* where each hour of your time costs a certain amount.

So, you need to measure your time and convert that to a dollar cost and then measure the leads / sales you are getting from the campaigns you are doing.

One of the principles that we assert here is that it's not about the next sale to a customer; rather a customer has (or should have) a lifetime value. That's the amount of revenue you'll generate from one customer over the lifetime of your engagement with them minus your costs to acquire them and then service them over time.

Let's say you're a mobile phone service provider and you know that the average customer spends $100 a month on your service. Over the course of 12 months, you generate $1,200 from the typical customer. But that customer doesn't stay with you for just 12 months, they stay with you for 3.5 years. The revenue you generate from them over the time that they remain your customer is $4,200 ($100/month x 12 months x 3.5 years).

There is a cost to service that customer each year for the time they remain your customer. Assume that each year this amounts to $30per month. The cost to service them over the span of time as your customer is $1,260 ($30/month x 12 months x 3.5 years).

The lifetime value calculation

In the most simple calculation, this would represent a customer lifetime value of the revenue generated by that customer over the 3.5 (or the average lifetime of a customer) years = $4,200 minus the cost to serve that customer over the 3.5 years = $2,940. If the cost of acquiring the customer is say 10% of customer lifetime value, you might spend close to $294 in marketing costs to gain a new customer. That's normally referred to in marketing texts as Cost Per Acquisition or sometimes called Cost Per Sale.

This is a good, basic formula for understanding the metrics of your social media ROI. Note however (as many business owners will already know) as a general rule of thumb for most businesses that it costs three to five times as much to get a new customer as it does to keep an existing one. That's part of the reason most businesses focus so much time and money on customer retention – it pays to keep existing customers happy.

Generating leads

As we noted earlier in the book, e-commerce is all about selling products over the Internet. It works for iTunes and Amazon very, very well. But what if you don't sell products online? What if you're a plumbing contractor or a business coach or a real estate agent? If that's the case, you're interested in generating leads, not sales.

In sales both online and offline, a lead is an inbound prospect who is interested in your product or service (or, as the case may be, in your competitor's product or service). If you can capture a lead and nurture it through the sales funnel, you'll be able to convert that prospect into a customer. And that means revenue for your business.

The Value of a Lead

To calculate your ROI when you don't directly sell online, you need to know the value of a lead to you. This is a very simple calculation. Take the number of leads generated over a given period and divide that by the number of new customers generated from those leads. Let's say in the past 12 months you have had 300 leads and 100 sales. Your lead conversion rate is 100/300 = 30%. If your lifetime value of a customer is $1000 then a lead is worth 30% of $1000 = $300. This means that every lead generated from your social media campaign is worth $300 to you.

But I Have a Business To Run!!!

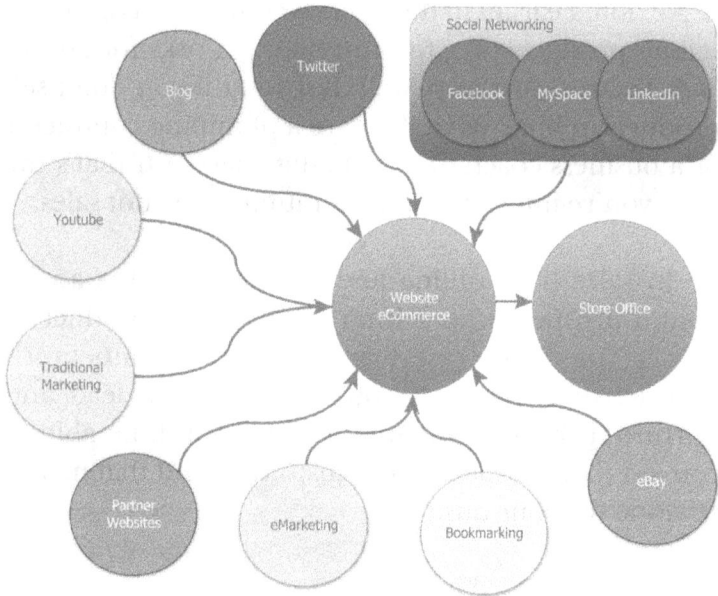

One of the issues that most small businesses will face when it comes to all of these aspects of social media and marketing possibilities is the issue of time. And that leads to a whole different discussion about outsourcing. What I suggest is not to try to do everything, but to try to do some things well.

The thing is, the average small business owner does not need to be on top of everything – in fact it's just not possible. What you should have is a strong strategy that encompasses three channels: search (websites and SEO), social media and email.

Search connects your business with people looking for what you are offering. Social media helps you go where your customers are and interact with them and email is direct marketing (and still the most effective means of communicating with your customers).

As far as social media is concerned, pick one or two elements and commit to a strategy to actually do them.

You need to put some time into creating a blog or to opening a Twitter account and posting regular Tweets or to creating a fan page on Facebook and then directing people back to your website from there.

If you try to do all of it, the sites will end up empty. Stay focused and consistent instead of trying to tackle it all. If you're going to create a blog, you need to commit to regular blog entries. And by regular, I don't mean daily or even weekly, but certainly one or two a month is a good idea to keep it fresh. Blogs are also very good for search engine optimisation, which we talked about in more detail in the SEO section.

Thus, once you're happy with your website, I would start out trialling one social media tool and use it regularly to see how it goes.

The other factor is that it also depends on who your customers are. If you are trying to appeal to a teenage market, then by all means get into Facebook and MySpace. Create a fan page and work that way.

If you're looking for business-to-business customers, you might find that LinkedIn is a good social networking site to use.

In both cases, you might be inclined to go with Twitter. But then again, it depends. If you're selling shoes at a local store then Twitter is not really going to be all that helpful for you.

If you're providing an advisory service, if you're an accountant or something like that, then Twitter could be very good because it will enable you to be positioned as an expert.

Thus, these are all the things you need to take into consideration when deciding what your online marketing strategy is. One of the key messages here is to realise that it takes time and that time shouldn't be wasted. Everything you do should be part of a marketing strategy and should be driven towards an increase in bottom line profit/revenue.

All these things we've been talking about are ultimately designed around making you money and you need to realise some sort of benefit from them.

If creating a blog and writing in it every day is not going to drive more people to your website and therefore drive more people to your sales then there's no point doing it. So you need to try to measure results. And we can talk in a different section about measurement of these types of things.

But the bottom line is you're trying to sell more things. By using social media it's more of a round-about route. You're trying to get people back to your key point of sale locations.

Cautionary Tales

You need to remember that what you put out there in the World Wide Web is out there for good and it can be transmitted many, many times, in many directions by many people. You must therefore, make sure that you never put anything out there of which you're not proud and confident.

For example, if you create a blog that takes a pot shot at one of your competitors, you might think that it's your own little blog and only a few people will see it. However, that blog can easily be transmitted by email, via other blogs, via Facebook or MySpace to a large audience and could get you into trouble. It could cause a lot of bad blood.

So you need to use these tools carefully. You need to protect against pushing your products too hard.

You need to use them to provide added value to the people who will be reading them. And then gently direct people back to your point-of-sale.

An example of a mistake on Facebook is the case of a guy who had called in sick to work, he had a terrible headache and wouldn't be in for work that day. Then he put on his Facebook page, "Excellent, I'm chucking a sickie. Now I'm off to the beach". He'd made one of his work colleagues a friend on Facebook and that information got back to his boss and he lost his job.

OMG I HATE MY JOB!! My boss is a total pervvy wanker always making me do shit stuff just to piss me off!! WANKER!
Yesterday at 18:03 · Comment · Like

Hi ⬤ i guess you forgot about adding me on here?
Firstly , don't flatter yourself. Secondly, you've worked here 5 months and didn't work out that i'm gay? I know i don't prance around the office like a queen, but it's not exactly a secret. Thirdly, that 'shit stuff' is called your 'job', you know, what i pay you to do. But the fact that you seem able to fuck-up the simplest of tasks might contribute to how you feel about it. And lastly, you also seem to have forgotten that you have 2 weeks left on your 6 month trial period. Don't bother coming in tomorrow. I'll pop your P45 in the post, and you can come in whenever you like to pick up any stuff you've left here. And yes i'm serious
Yesterday at 22:53

write a comment..

Hence, you have to be careful with Facebook and the risk of the merging personal and business lives. You can be a very well respected, well dressed, well presented person and well known in your local network for being professional and serious. But all it takes is one photo on Facebook of you driving the porcelain bus and your reputation can be shot to pieces.

An example of a Twitter mistake was made by media-savvy people who worked at confectionary brand Skittles. Instead of building their own website they redirected the Skittles.com website to a Twitter search results page. The idea was that everybody would go to the page and see everybody Tweeting about Skittles. What the Skittles people hadn't prepared for was pranksters to flood the Tweets with remarks about the brand, such as, "Skittles got stuck in my mouth while I was driving, forcing me to slam into an orphanage, killing hundreds. I'll never eat them again."

Things You May Not Have Looked At

CRM Systems

Ancient Chinese warrior Sun Tzu says, "Know your enemy". Good business owners say, "Know your clients".

You can't know your clients properly without a CRM – customer relationship management system. They're essential to the effective running of a business. A CRM can take on many forms. For some people, it's simply a contact list; for others, it's a large software application, with thousands of pieces of information on their clients.

These days, there are many good, low-cost solutions that can allow small business owners to operate like bigger businesses. To start understanding the value of a CRM, ask a few questions... Do you know where your customers live? Do you know their postcode or geographic area? Do you know the demographic of your customers? Are they in a higher or lower earning range? Are they a certain nationality? What gender are they? Knowing this will help you market yourself in the non-Internet world.

Do you know what your lead-to opportunity conversion rate is? If you know this, you can work backwards and identify how many leads you need in order to make money. Do you know what the cost of a lead is to you? For every lead you get, if you're paying nearly as much as the amount you get from that lead, then you have a problem.

Do you know the value of a lead? This is very important, yet a lot of people don't know this. If you can put a dollar value on a lead it gives you more motivation because often you'll discover that the value of one lead may be worth $300 to you or $1000. Thus, whenever anyone tells you they'd like you to meet someone who may be interested in your product or service, then you can immediately ascertain how much it's worth to you. If it's going to be worth $500, you're motivated to go meet with those people to try to convert the lead into a sale.

Benefits of a CRM

Of all the several benefits of having a CRM system, the most important is maintaining a contact list. This is essential if you want to market to your existing customers. From there, you can manage the actual *relationship* with your customers if it's relevant to your business. For example, call and mail logging – i.e. when your customer rings you, you talk to them on the phone and you both promise something, which can then be noted in your CRM system.

This is helpful in those situations when the customer comes back to you and tells you, "But you said 'this' six weeks ago in a phone conversation", and you can't remember it. CRM solves these types of issues. It also manages your sales pipeline – your leads and your opportunities. Too many people run their businesses on a day-to-day basis. They see what comes in the door today – maybe they made money, maybe they didn't – and they're not sure what's coming in tomorrow. A good sales pipeline is essential. You can see months forward and you can see when sales are going to dip and you can do something about it, giving yourself enough time to take action.

A lot of CRM systems now will allow you to do quoting and invoicing. So once again, you're trying to get this full system around your customer with all the information that's relevant to them.

You can also track purchase dates and amounts. Who are your best customers? Which customers have the most value to you? And which ones don't? Which ones make lots of phone calls to you but don't actually buy very much? They might make a lot of noise, but financially they're not very valuable.

Know your customer

An interesting example about knowing your customers came about a few years ago with the Sony PlayStation. Sony, for a long time, thought that its customer was a 16- or 17-year-old male who wanted to play a lot of shoot-'em-up and car racing-style games. That was partly true. There were a lot of customers like that, but then Sony decided to do a study into who its customer really was.

The result was surprising. In fact, the actual age of its customers was much higher than initially believed. They had a very large demographic in the late twenties, early thirties who enjoyed playing PlayStation, and who had a larger disposable income so they could buy more games. They also discovered that about 30 per cent of these customers were women, which is a really important demographic to understand because that changes the entire way that you market your product as well as the products you supply. Then Sony started bringing out games better suited to that older age group and that would entice women as well.

Understanding your customer demographic is essential and you cannot do that without a decent CRM system.

Another good example started out on Amazon.com but is now repeated a lot of websites. When you go to look at a particular product or buy something, at the bottom of the web page you'll see examples of "People who bought this product, also bought ...". This is a type of CRM because it helps you understand your customers' buying patterns, and track and analyse the results.

Types of CRM systems

There are a lot of different types, so we'll break them into four main categories.

First is the out of the box variety. This is PC-based software that you purchase from a vendor. For example, ACT is a very popular contact management system. QuickBooks and Myob finance tools provide some level of contact management. Another one is Goldmine.

The second type is a custom-based PC solution. That's having somebody build you something, which is obviously a lot more expensive but will enable you to get exactly what you want.

The third type is a web-based out of the box solution. Examples of these are Sugar CRM (www.sugar-crm.com),Info At Hand (www.infoathand.com),Zoho (www.zoho.com), Salesforce (www.salesforce.com), FreeCRM (www.freecrm.com). As out of the box systems, they cannot be customized, so you use the system as is.

The fourth one is the customised web-based solution. This is again more expensive but you get exactly what you want. It's built to your business specifications. For small businesses that are just starting out, I would suggest a web-based out-of-the-box solution – something like Zoho which is a good one and inexpensive.

Contact and interaction management

When you're analysing which one to use, try to break down what you want to get out of it. First of all, all of them will provide you with **contact management** – basically, being able to store your contact details in the database and access them easily. Then, look at actual **interaction management** – being able to track phone calls, emails to and from, taking note of when follow-ups occur. This is an excellent way to know what has gone on between you and that client, and how long the sales process is taking. If you're in a service-based business where you quote and then follow-up, do you have to follow-up two times on average or six or seven times before you get a definitive yes or no answer?

Sales pipeline management

Sales pipeline management is essential, particularly if you're in a service-based industry where you are quoting and you do have the full pipeline (it's a little less relevant for retail-based business). Managing your leads and opportunities and knowing your conversion rates is very important. If these things are relevant to you, you need that in your CRM.

Invoicing and quoting: you may already have some sort of invoicing or quoting system but once again, if you can find a system that incorporates all these functions it's very helpful. For example, if a customer phones you to inquire about an invoice, you can very quickly access the information required.

Issue management

As much as we may like to think we won't have issues, we invariably do and if you're in a business where your customers will phone you with a problem, you need to log that issue. It's very important because if you log it, you can track it and process it correctly and efficiently. Plus, you can work out how long it's taking you to track and process it.

You can provide the customer with a feedback mechanism on your website or via an email and see which customers have had the most problems. Plus, you can see which product or service is generating the most issues. You can then make informed decisions about how to resolve the issues.

If you're in a business where the purchase of your product or service requires a process in order to fulfil that purchase – for example, if you're providing a service that's a small project–you need some kind of order and project management so you know when it started and when the customer paid their first invoice. You can track the steps you need to take and assign tasks to people in order to bring the project to completion.

Campaign management

One of the reasons you want to have your contacts in a database is so you can market to them. A campaign management system helps you to dissect your customer base. For example, you only want the people in a particular suburb who have bought a particular product in the past six months because you want to do a letterbox drop. Or, you want to know all the people over the age of 55 because you want to send them an email telling them about a new seminar you're running.

There are other things you can look for, such as supplier management, if you do a lot of purchase orders.

From a financial perspective, many small businesses don't have the money to spend, but it's important to be aware of critically important investments. The CRM system is one of those because it can do so much for your business.

That said, you don't need to spend a lot. You can start out with a cheap or a free solution and see how that goes, but you might find you need to move on to a custom solution or to one of the more sophisticated out-of-the-box solutions. Generally speaking, I would argue towards a web solution because you can access it anywhere and you can build add-ons to it – such as a customer portal, whereby your customers can get access to some of this information themselves if this is relevant.

Maintaining a CRM

We've talked about websites in the past and keeping them fresh and constantly working on them; a CRM system is the same. You can't just buy and implement a CRM system and then not put any effort into it. You absolutely need to keep it updated and it needs to become part of your business process.

For example, when you acquire a new customer or when you're handed a business card by someone at an event, you should have a process in place that gets that information into your CRM system. You should also have some standards about how you enter that information into your CRM system to keep the data accurate. There's no point having someone in your CRM system with no postcode or no street address if you're planning on posting them information in the future. Obviously, you always need to try to have email addresses and phone numbers in the correct fields and have a system to update the CRM when a client changes their details.

Try to keep your data valid because these types of systems can get very out-of-hand if you're just putting rubbish into them. As they say, "rubbish in, rubbish out", and the same holds true for CRMs.

When customers raise an issue with you, you also need to put that in the CRM system. Even if it's a small problem to fix and it's quick and simple to resolve, it should still be logged. Following a process like this is important because that same small problem may arise for someone else, so you'll already have a resolution in place and logged. Although it may only take five minutes to fix, if you're getting the same problem five times a day it's something that needs to be addressed and you need to be tracking that.

Using the CRM to help you

Then use this information to analyse your business. We've had clients who've done a lot of work on their CRM, set up their processes, the data's in and it's all perfect but then they don't look at it. They never take that extra step to start analysing the information. Ultimately it's all about analysing that data to gain an insight into your customers' behaviours in order to come up with new ways to market and sell to them and to market and sell to new customers based on the information you've obtained from your existing ones.

Finally, you need to take some time every month or every quarter to analyse your data and see where your money is coming from and who are your best customers; what market segment or products are the highest performing; what your leads ratios are, etc.

When implementing a CRM system, if you work in a business with more than just yourself as an employee, you have to remember to train your staff. One of the biggest ways for a new piece of software to fail is a lack of understanding, training and acceptance by the employees.

With a CRM system, which could be a core component of your business, it's essential that your employees understand why you're putting it in place, what benefit it will give to your business and that they know how to use it. You need to train staff and provide them with information – cheat sheets or a manual – and encourage them to ask questions if they're not sure of anything. Let them know that you prefer them to ask questions rather than input the data incorrectly.

In summary, business generally speaking is about building and maintaining relationships – and that's what a CRM system is. It can build and maintain relationships. It can also help you with your efficiency and enable you to market more effectively to your existing and potential customers.

SaaS – Software As A Service

The way in which we purchase and use software is changing. No so long ago, we were obliged to purchase a version of a popular software product that we needed for several hundreds or thousands of dollars and then pay each time we wanted an upgrade. That software was installed on a single machine and lots unscrupulous people spent their time working out how to pirate the software to get it onto other machines without having to purchase a new licence.

There were often issues with compatibility and we were often locked into upgrades when the software we had was no longer compatible with the operating system to which we wanted to upgrade.

With the rise of the Internet and improvement in our connection speeds, we have started developing a raft of web applications (see more about this in the Web Application section) to replace the software on our PC's. Not only are we starting to see online software, but there has been a major shift in the way we pay for it. We now have Software As A Service. This means that we pay a monthly subscription fee for the software (e.g. $29 per month for project management software) which allows us to use it from anywhere we have an internet connection.

Analyst Robert DeSisto of Gartner predicts that software revenue generated by SaaS products is to increase to 25% by the year 2011. This would be up from 5% of market share in 2005.

The Gartner report sees SaaS vendors moving from the just "good enough" phase of products that came out during2000-2003 to a new breed of application that is now easier to use and more highly customisable. But adoption varies significantly by application type/market segment.

Salesforce.com is still considered the best example of a successful SaaS implementation. Salesforce. com Q2 2007 financials show that they have 500,000 subscribers and are on their way to $489 million in revenues for 2007, rapid growth considering they had 100,000 subscribers in 2004 and $87 million in revenue.

The benefits of SaaS can be enormous. The obvious is the flexibility of having your office software wherever you go. You also have the concept of fixed IT costs. Instead of waiting for the next upgrade, holding off as long as possible, having issues with file versions and compatibility, we have an alternative where we always have the latest version, no file version issues and a lot fewer compatibility issues for a fixed price per month – no surprises.

The original software as a service (even before the term was coined) was Hotmail and the other mail tools around at that time. Now most types of software are out there from office products (Google Docs is trying to compete with the Microsoft suite and Microsoft themselves are releasing online versions of their software), as well as things such as accounting packages. Note that QuickBooks and MYOB – the two main accounting packages for small business in Australia – do not yet (as at 2010) have online versions of their software, although MYOB is very close.

Accountant, Mark Lehman spotted an opportunity a number of years ago to apply the SaaS to his world, providing accounting software packages to SMEs. He claims his business, Saasu, an online accounting software company with over 10,000 customers, is Australia's largest. "It's a web based service available on a pay-as-you-go basis."

Saasu is a comprehensive online accounting software system for managing business financials including sales reporting, purchasing, inventory, payroll, e-commerce. Its applications enable connection you to have up to hundreds of web applications, software products, payment services and banks. Lehman says, "With cloud computing you just pay a monthly fee of $25 and you get updates, upgrades and ongoing service. It's a departure from the traditional model which involved a capital expenditure upfront. It (the cloud) allows us to buy much more expensive and powerful technology and recover our investment over time in very small payments from many users.

"You get a lot more value for your subscription without the upfront investment (because we have already made that investment on your behalf)."

Another business, Ourtel operates its home-based call centre capability so all its operators (about 10 to 15) are spread across multiple locations. Managing director Ruth McKay, says her virtual call centre has workers spread around the world. As a small business owner she is able to offer big business solutions. "We've only been in business 18 months and are able to compete with some of the larger contact centre providers. We offer clients high calibre, remote based tele-agents who provide customer care and phone support. We've only a small head office.

"We pay the IP provider (such as IPscape) on an as-need subscription basis and we get cutting edge technology. Typically, we'll do a campaign for a charity; doing their outbound calls. The client gives us the list of names; this is sent to the service provider who uploads the information, enabling each of our (remote) agents to key into the password-protected URL and work off the screen. It's a powerful resource and offers instant metrics and reports. Real time reports are a competitive edge for us. The client wants to know how their campaign is going. Our agent could be in Toowoomba or in Auckland; it makes no difference."

She says that the issues of supervision and control do not present problems as she is able to access an untapped market of high calibre candidates that traditionally would not consider working in a call centre environment. "The technology is the key."

"The traditional contact centre model doesn't always work. The quality of agents was often dubious – unreliable. You only attracted transient students. In the virtual model we attract people who are talented but who may not have been able to come in to a call centre. They may be parents wanting to return to the workforce, retired professionals, people that live in remote locations, people with disabilities, people only wanting to work flexible hours."

She says the maturity factor is very important for not for profit sector clients. "These people appreciate the privilege of working from home."

It also offers lower barriers to entry for trials. "It gives the NFP the ability to test our capabilities at a low entry cost. It would be hard to do this with some of the larger contact centres. The cost benefit works out favourably around 15 agents; this is where the technology is so wonderful. It enables smaller, niche operators like us to be competitive and thrive."

Instant Messaging

Many of you will have used some type of instant message tool – Skype, MSN, AOL. Many of us use these tools for social interaction. Some businesses are taking advantage of this technology for commercial purposes.

In 2008 I was in Shanghai, China. Staying with a friend; we were hungry and they pulled out a book with hundreds of restaurants in it, complete with menus and prices. There was a single business that put out the book and managed the customer interaction – and it was all done via MSN. We simply connected to them via msn, gave them numbers from the book (any restaurant) and they did the rest. We managed to get a combination of Indian, Mexican and traditional Chinese, without a phone call, email or any communication form except chatting. It was instantaneous customer service, and the food arrived quickly.

While this is not suitable as a total solution for many businesses (and nor would you want it to be), it may be an interesting alternative communication channel with your customers.

One interesting piece of technology is the ability to place a small piece of code onto your website that is integrated with your chat application. Then, when someone browses to your site, your chat is automatically activated and you can effectively do what people do in physical stores – you can ask, "Can I help you with something?" The users screen pops up the message and they can start to chat with you if they want.

In my technology business I communicate a lot with clients in other parts of Australia or the world via chat. It is fast and efficient, but as usual there are some gotchas.

Chat is a very instant and informal means of communication. This has a couple of problems – the first is that your clients may feel that they have your attention on tap – and you may get into a situation where 20 times a day, a client quickly chats with you to ask for some information which can be very inefficient for your own time management. The second major issue is the informality of it. I have had the situation where a client has asked for something via chat, like, "When you get a chance, can you update...?" If during a busy day with lots of chats and emails and phone calls, if you have not noted this action in your To Do list, it can quickly scroll off the screen and be forgotten – only to have the client remind you at a future date (and be able to retrieve the proof of having asked you).

So, instant messages aren't for everyone, but they have some definite benefits, particularly in making you accessible to customers, creating informal communication lines and increasing efficiency of customer service. If you can manage the downsides with some good procedures for the use of chatting, I recommend it.

RSS Feeds

RSS (Rich Site Summary) is **a format for delivering regularly changing web content**. Many news-related sites, weblogs and other online publishers syndicate their content as an **RSS Feed** to whoever wants it. The purpose is to enable readers to subscribe to a feed and have it delivered to them rather than having to open a webpage to view it.

You need an RSS reader program (there are about 5 million of these). Microsoft Outlook can actually accept RSS feeds, so that is one option.

The benefit to your business is relatively limited. If you are a publisher of content (as you should be) you could provide RSS feeds on your blog for example.

This would enable people to subscribe to your blog feed and not have to visit your blog. The benefit here is that they may be more likely to read your posts.

Generally speaking I think there are many other technologies in this book that are better suited to improving your bottom line.

Twitter Me Dead!

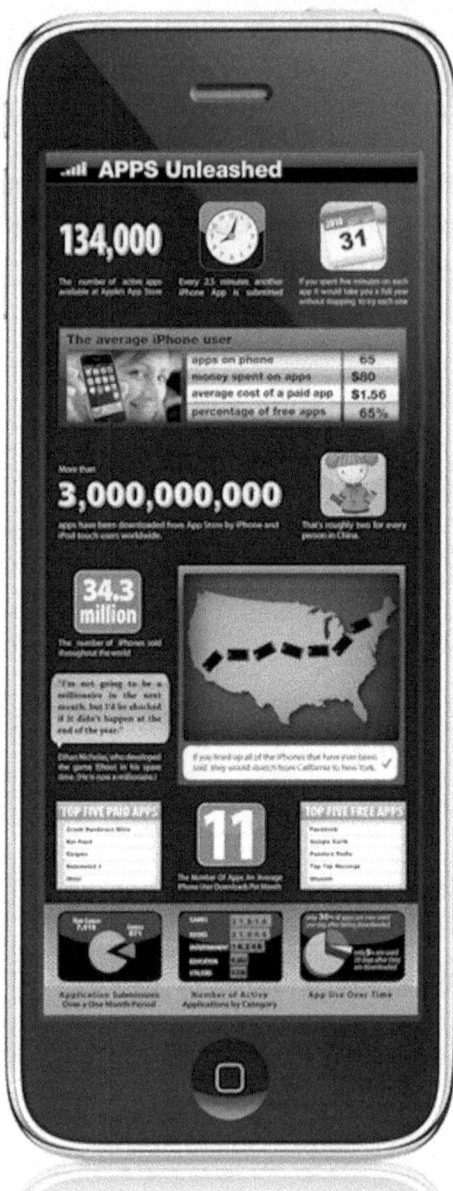

iPhone Apps

Do you have an iPhone? If you do, you are part of the 24% of mobile phone users that have one. It seems that everywhere you look, someone has an iPhone. One of the reasons that these phones have become so incredibly popular in a short space of time is not just that they are Apple branded or well designed, but also that they have the App Store. This in an online store accessed from your phone where you can download FREE or almost free applications. And the beauty is that there is an app for almost anything. Need to order a pizza, reserve a movie ticket, use a spirit level, get painting advice for your house, create a song....it's all there, allowing the iPhone to be the equivalent of a Swiss army knife.

While the iPhone led the way, there is strong competition from Google Android and Nokia – with very similar apps. Even Microsoft is trying to stay in the game with their latest offering.

The reason that all these players are trying to be involved in the mobile and mobile app business is that they see this as a serious money spinner moving over the next decade. This is where we need to ask the questions, "What about small business? And what's in it for us?"

Well, how about this?

1. **New targeted advertising opportunities**
   - Consumers who download certain applications are showing their interest in that

area – meaning that if your business services that area in some way, then these people are you target market.

2. **Ability to offer a free value added service to your clients**
   - Not for everyone, but is there an application that your customers may want that you could provide them? If you supply fishing products, your clients will be interested in the tidal tables, moon phases and info on which fish like what lures. Imagine an application where your business sponsors an app for that.

3. **Ability to sell your products via a NEW stream – not web, not shopfront, but mobile**
   - Move into the advertising market. If you have a large customer base, and can think of something that your customers may want in the way of a mobile application, then you now have a means of selling advertising to other suppliers in the same area. This can provide a whole new revenue stream.[7]

Location Based Services

Location Based Services is something that you will be hearing more and more about. It's the merging of advertising information with geographic location information and GPS location of your mobile device.

---

7   Source: www.newmaconline.com 28th Jan 2010

Basically it means you can ask your phone where the nearest ATM machine is or the nearest place to get a pizza and it will spit out GPS-based local results. Based on your current location it will list businesses in the immediate area that match your search.

Some examples of location based services are:

- Recommending social events in a city
- Requesting the nearest business or service, such as an ATM or restaurant
- Turn by turn navigation to any address
- Locating people on a map displayed on the mobile phone
- Receiving alerts, such as notification of a sale on shoes or warning of a traffic jam
- Location-based mobile advertising

What does this mean for you? Well it means that if your business is the sort of business that would benefit from being found in a location based search, then you should be in it.

Note that at the moment, based on research done by the Pew Research Centre[8], 7% of adults who go online with their mobile device use location based services. So the numbers are still quite low, but this industry is really very young and the next few years will see it explode.

---

8   Pew Internet and American Life Project Nov 2010

eBay

eBay first started in 1995 (seems like yesterday) as AuctionWeb by Pierre Omidyar. One of the first items sold on eBay was a broken laser pointer for $14.83. Astonished, Omidyar contacted the winning bidder to ask if he understood that the laser pointer was broken. In his responding email, the buyer explained: "I'm a collector of broken laser pointers."[9] From this point on, Omidyar knew he was onto something.

eBay is currently valued at USD$36.11 billion[10]– that's a lot of broken laser pointers.

eBayers are an eclectic bunch. They're different too from the traditional flea market participants who tend to be more interested in small change trading. Ebay sits neatly between the traditional second hand dealer and the cooler eBay savvy trader. eBayers range from teenagers hunting down vintage clothing to computer gamers to music. Many are collectors or hobbyists and therefore know a thing or two about their particular passion, and their expertise, allied to the Internet, can turn a hobby into a business as it grows and more serious dealing is taking place. Pianos, cars, and broken laser pointers – almost anything is being traded.

The business of doing business on eBay is booming.

According to a July 2009 survey conducted by eBay, more than 724,000 Americans and a reported 100,000

9 How did eBay start?, About.com. Retrieved on 2007-01-26.
10 Finance.yahoo.com

Australians say that eBay is their primary or second-ary source of income. In addition to these professional eBay sellers, another 1.5 million individuals say they supplement their income by selling on eBay.

Over 50,000 people in the UK draw a significant portion of their income from selling goods online. A study by the Centre for Economics and Business Research shows that the average household boosts its earnings by GBP 3,000 through online trading.

eBay is far and away the most popular of the in-ternet-based dealers in second hand groups. Amazon follows closely behind but its range of goods is mainly around books and DVDs, but also extends to car parts and electrical goods.

Everyone has heard of someone raking in six-figure incomes from a spare bedroom equipped with a PC, an Internet connection and a digital camera. They call this a virtual store. With just a computer and an Internet connection, virtually anyone these days can start their own website and market their products and services from home without spending a lot of money. It seems more on the Internet means more traders and dealers in the real world.

You do have to wonder at the fact that the Internet has made geography irrelevant. Think of something – anything–and you will find it on eBay. And it's a mar-ketplace that is so deep and so wired, it allows for price information to be totally arbitraged. That means any difference in price is an opportunity for the quick on-line trader because within minutes the price will be levelled. No longer can there be any doubt about what something is worth, whatever it is.

Many private individuals use eBay to buy and sell all types of goods. As noted above, some people even make a business out of selling items on eBay. Assuming that you are not interested in dumping your existing business and going into selling WWII German Army Helmets (of which there were 112 available at last check), then you may be thinking that eBay is not for you. If you are an e-tailer (online retailer), then you have a couple of options with eBay that may be interesting.

Bait and Switch: Remembering that one of our prin-ciple aims is to draw potential clients to our website, you can place selected items on eBay and then making sure that you advertise your real site in your About Me page. In the past, eBay allowed you to link directly to your site from the description of your item, but that has now changed. However you can direct people to your About Me page on eBay and from there, direct them to your site. The end result is that you can get more people coming to your site whether or not they purchased the original item. The double benefit here is that not only will you sell more, but these extra links to your site will help your SEO ranking.

Double Offensive: For people who wish to sell a lot of goods on eBay, you can actually open an eBay shop.

This is effectively an online store for your eBay products – whether they are buy now items (no auction) or auction items. You have the ability to personalise your shop, add your logo, change colours and even have your own domain name. However, eBay is as swamped as the rest of the Internet and having your own shop is hard work (especially if you also have an eCommerce site). eBay recommends that you are a high volume seller first and are committed to growing your eBay store. Once you have it, you also need to market it in a similar way to marketing your own website. Learn more about eBay stores at http://pages.ebay.com/help/sell/store-getstarted.html.

If you are a hard core retailer (or e-tailer) then you are probably already using / know of eBay. One of the benefits of eBay is that you can run auctions and specials to a relatively captive audience, so it's definitely worth being involved in. However before jumping into a full blown eBay store, I would focus on your eCommerce site and use eBay to help get more traffic to that (as well as selling a few items).

What's coming.....?

No one of course truly knows what is coming – even the experts. A great example of this is our current world-wide Internet problem with IP addresses (these are the unique 12 digit numbers that identify every device on the Internet – 188.231.45.10 – every web address that you go to has one of these numbers behind it). In 1977 when the pioneers of the Internet dreamed up the concept of IP addresses, they were confident that 4.2 billion combinations were definitely enough to last the next 100 years or more. 33 years later we have run out. The internet is full. Even the absolute visionaries of that time, got it way wrong about how much the Internet would be used. They never in their wildest dreams thought about phones connecting to the Internet (let alone TV's, fridges, watches, cars...).

So, all of that to say that the following is a best guess for the near term and is likely to be way off target. By the way, the new internet addressing (when it finally gets setup) called IPv6 can cater for about 230 trillion trillion trillion addresses – that should last us a while - shouldn't it?

Everything Connected – Internet Enabled Devices

Leading on from talk of internet address shortages is one of the safest predictions I can make. Everything (I mean everything) will be connected to the Internet in some form or another. The reason for this is control. We want to have control over everything from any-where. Some examples of what we can do and what we will be able to do are here:

- Merging of the hardware and the Internet data. For example, the new Garmin Nuvi GPS uses local based service info to get you to the nearest hardware store.
- You can already control your air-conditioner from your web enabled mobile phone
- Your fridge will be able to automatically order food when its run out or tell what is out of date
- Your car will be online, and your engine system can be monitored in real time by your mechan-ic, who charges you an annual maintenance fee to monitor it and make real time tweaks

Everything Online – Cloud Computing

As we read earlier, the point of cloud computing is that instead of using a single computer in a single location to store and process data, we use an abstract object called the cloud that is in effect any number of comput-ers in any number of locations all working together to do something. The beauty of it for us is that we don't care about where it is, what it is or how it works. What we care about is *that it works* and how much it costs.

You are probably already using the cloud even without knowing it. Ever bought a book from Amazon.com? Ever used Google's Gmail? These are both in the cloud.

As we move forward more and more things will move into the cloud – including the actual software we use and our own very personal very private data.

Software online

Even today, if you wanted to, you could throw away those software CD's in the corner, and clear Microsoft Office from your personal computer, and not suffer any real drop in productivity. This is because both Microsoft and Google provide online office productivity software that you access through a web browser.

Take a look at:
Google Docs - https://docs.google.com
Office Live - https://login.live.com/

Soon, we will no longer need to have office servers with expensive software and licences that are tied to a single machine. We won't need the tape drive next to the server that does the backups. Instead we will use our software online. Microsoft Word will be run from a web browser and we will be paying a monthly fee (or perhaps pay per use) for access to it. We will store our files online and pay monthly for space used which will include backups. Our accounting software will be online and will integrate automatically with our online banking. Sharing a document will be as simple as pointing someone to it and giving access – in fact we will probably be working on a single copy of a document together at the same time.

Data online

Of course if our software is online, our data will also be online. Not just a few Word documents, but all of it. Our payroll information, banking details, personal photographs, travel itineraries – all of it.

We will be paying for the disk space that we use, and it will be managed for us. Sophisticated backup software will make sure that our data is secure (for a price). We won't know exactly where it is (the US, Australia, Ecuador – or all of these) but we will be able to access it all from wherever we are – in the car, on the train or in a hotel in Tasmania (yes, even from Tasmania).

Massive data

One of the opportunities (and challenges) of storing all the worlds data in the cloud is the sheer enormity of that data. If you think it is hard to find things now on Google, just wait!

The possibilities for medical and scientific research are huge. Imagine being able to store massive amounts of data and then being able to throw massive amounts of computing power at it on a scale never before seen in order to solve scientific problems. This is really exciting!

However for the average business person running the average business, the trick will be not to get drowned in information. An entire industry will emerge in data evaluation and data mining and knowledge management – experts who will be able to trawl the world's data in order to provide you what you need.

Mobile computing

The computing devices that we currently know will continue to evolve rapidly and some of our preconceived notions will be challenged. Who would have thought even 10 years ago, that with a single handheld device you could do all of the following:

- Make and receive phone calls
- Send TXT messages
- Surf the Internet
- Tell the time
- Provide a weather forecast
- Play, store and share music
- Control the TV
- Read the news
- Take photos and videos
- Edit photos and videos

- Keep the family budget and share it with your partner
- Access your bank
- Play games
- Navigate using a GPS

Of course the current crop of advanced mobile devices can do this and a lot more. Led by the iPhone and equally importantly the iPhone App Store, these devices are, in a word, breathtaking. It's hard to imagine where they can go from here, but they will continue to grow in power and application. The need for a PC on the desk at home has been and will continue to diminish (and perhaps disappear altogether). The idea of doing some work at the computer will change. Our work, social, connected and unconnected time will merge into one. Instead of doing a few hours in front of the computer and then watching TV, we will be emailing while we are driving home (using voice recognition of course), checking messages on our mobile device as we come inside, taking a quick video chat on our TV before we stream the movie we want to watch from the Internet, and monitoring the football results from our iPad while we are watching it and waiting for the pizza that we ordered online.

Mouse? What Mouse?

In the ever changing world of computing, two things have been relatively static – the keyboard and the mouse.

The first rollerball mouse was invented in 1972 and really has not changed that much. The technology has changed a little – using infrared light rather than a roller ball (although you can still get those), and some are wireless, but the basic concept is the same – move the mouse with your hand across the desk and it controls the pointer on the screen.

Aside: Many years ago I was teaching an Introduction to Computing class for a TAFE College in Central Australia. I had a class of middle aged public servants who had been told they needed to learn computers. To start the first lesson, I wanted to ease people into it, and knowing that they had no knowledge, I thought we would start with a nice drawing program to get used to using the mouse. I instructed the class to move the mouse to the top right hand corner of the screen. To my amazement, one person physically picked up the mouse and held it against the top right hand corner of the computer monitor and then turned to look at me waiting patiently for the next instruction.

Recently the concepts of the mouse and keyboard have been challenged in a number of ways.

- The advent of touch screen monitors provides the possibility to touch and drag on the actual screen itself. While this is great for interactive displays and maps of shopping centres I do not believe it will be useful for general computing as it is not ergonomically comfortable *with the current computer monitors.*
- Tablet PC's have been around for a while, but the iPad has led the way bringing them into the mainstream. With a tablet PC, using the screen as your pointing device makes perfect sense and is very intuitive.
- Voice recognition – over the past 5-10 years, major advances have been made in voice recognition. At the start you needed to train the computer to understand your commands by speaking it 50 times first. Now you can simply talk and most software has a pretty good accuracy. Voice recognition is only going to improve and I suspect will cause the death of the keyboard.
- Mousepads, trackpads or touchpads have been in laptops for many years now as alternative pointing devices. Once again it was Apple who revolutionised them with the multi touch mousepad for the MacBook laptop range. By allowing multi touch, the utility of mousepads has been increased enormously. Now you can use two fingers to resize and rotate images, three fingers to change applications, swiping move-

ments to flick between documents or images etc. This has proven so popular that they have just released a large version for their non-laptop range that is designed specifically to replace the mouse. The jury is still out on this but I suspect this will be a real challenger to the mouse.

No Such Thing As A Free Lunch

Don't you just love free? I do. And more than anything in history, the Internet has spawned this amazing concept of just giving stuff away. At least that is what it seems. Take a closer look though and you will see that nothing is really free. There is always a reason. The early days of computing and the Internet were probably the most altruistic. Computer geeks gave away their code and the cool things to other computer geeks for free – to help out and if we are to be honest to be paid in kudos. Since then we have continued to give things away for free:

- Sometimes for data (give us your email address, answer a few questions)
- Sometimes for a short time – free trial or the more devious concept of getting a following using some software and when people are committed to it, hit them with a fee
- Sometimes as a tickler – you can have the free version of this great game, but you can only advance two levels and then you need to pay
- Sometimes it's free but full of advertising

There are many gotchas in the free concept. I think that these days most people realise this, but nonetheless we have become used to it. In effect we are happy to trade something (usually our data) to get free things. The classic example of this is Facebook. A massive application requiring enormous resources to run – and yet it's free. Why? Well advertising of course – and not just advertising, but *targeted* advertising based on what we do and what we type.

That said, there is a push back towards the old school dirty approach of asking for money for your services. The two most common in the new technology world are:

Subscriptions: Paying a small fee per month (e.g. $12-$30) for access to a website or an online piece of software. There are typically no contracts or commitments, you just sign up and leave when you want.

Micropayments: This has become hugely popular with iTunes and then the iPhone. Imagine paying 69c for a song or $1.19 for a game. At the same time Microsoft is trying to sell games for the Xbox at $120! Micropayments are extremely clever. There has always been a general marketing / business rule of thumb that the more you charge, the more value your product or service will be perceived to have. There are countless stories of business people doubling and tripling the price of their offering and at the same time increasing sales. Micropayments have gone totally the other way. By making the price so close to $0 (free), people perceive the item that way and purchase automatically. There is very little buying thought taking place, "It's only a $1.19, who cares if it's no good – I'll just delete it." In this way, while the $1.19 goes nowhere near covering the cost of the application, the fact that it is so cheap means that thousands if not millions of people will buy and volume will provide profit.

I think that over the coming years we will find ourselves happily paying small amounts for things that previously we saw as our right to be provided free.

Final Note - Don't Get Carried Away

As I mentioned in the introduction, I understand totally the time pressures on small businesses. It will be virtually impossible for you to undertake all or probably even half of the ideas in this book at one time and still do the important work of running your business. So, I urge you to take a steady, planned approach to your online presence.

The first point is really having a solid and presentable website that turns viewers into sales or leads with a reasonable conversion. If you can get to that stage, then you are already ahead of most businesses out there.

Next, choose one or two of the drivers that can help direct people to your site. This may be a LinkedIn profile or a Facebook page or some email marketing. If a blog suits your business then that can help in a number of ways as well. Take your time, be methodical, experiment and then measure. You will find that some things don't work for you and hopefully others work really well. Then you will see where to focus your time.

Glossary of Terms

A/B Testing - In A/B testing, you unleash two different versions of a keyword, advertisement, website, web/landing page, banner design or variable and see which performs the best. You test version A vs. version B to see how different versions perform.

Above the fold
With reference to the top part of a newspaper, the term is used in Internet marketing to describe the top part of the page that the user can see without scrolling down.

Account Daily Spending Limit
Maximum amount you want to spend each day. You may be charged up to 10% above your Account Daily Spending Limit.

Ad Clicks
Number of times users click on an ad banner.

Ad Groups - A group of ads within a Campaign. A set of ads and related keywords within a campaign. The ads can be displayed to prospective customers searching for or viewing content related to your keywords and/or ads. You can apply a default ad group bid to all keywords in an ad group or set custom bids for individual keywords.

Ad Group Bid
The default bid you set to apply to keywords in an ad group. You can override the ad group bid for a keyword by setting a custom keyword bid.

Address
A unique identifier for a computer or site online, usually a URL for a web site or marked with an @ for an email address. Literally, it is how your computer finds a location on the information highway.

Analytics
A feature that allows you to understand a wide range of activity related to your website and your online marketing activities. Using analytics provides you with information to help optimize your campaigns, ad groups, and keywords, as well as your other online marketing activities, to best meet your business goals.

B2B
Business to Business

B2C
Business to Consumer

Bandwidth
How much information (text, images, video, and sound) can be sent through a connection. Usually measured in bits-per-second. A full page of text is about 16,000 bits. A fast modem can move approximately 15,000 bits in one second. Full-motion full-screen

video requires about 10,000,000 bits-per-second, depending on compression.

Backlinks
Backlinks are incoming links to a webpage. Backlinks are important for search engine optimization (SEO) because some search engines, give more credit to websites that have a good number of quality backlinks. Sites with better backlink counts usually rank better in SERPs

Banner
Banners are the 468-by-60 pixels ad space on commercial Web sites that are usually "hot-linked" to the advertiser's site.

Bid
The maximum amount that you are willing to pay for a click.

Bid Adjustments
A percentage or a fixed monetary amount by which to increase a bid for cases where traffic appears to be consistent with your selected targeting preferences. This is an optional feature that you can use to more competitively bid for certain targets.

Bid Limit
When campaign optimization is turned on, the bid limit defines the maximum amount that you are willing to pay for a click.
Black Hat SEO - Those who practice search engine optimization with unethical methods.

Blog - A blog is an online journal or "log" of any given subject. Blogs are easy to update, manage, and syndicate, powered by individuals and/or corporations and enable users to comment on postings.

Bookmark

A bookmark is an easy way to find your way Back to a web site – just like a real bookmark helps you keep your place in a book you are reading.

Bot

Abbreviation for robot (also called a spider). It refers to software programs that scan the web. Bots vary in purpose from indexing web pages for search engines to harvesting e-mail addresses for spammers

Bounce Rate - This shows a percentage of entrances on any given page that resulted in an exit from the page without entering any other page on the site.

Branding

A school of advertising that says, "If the consumer has heard of us, we've done our job." Fortunately for agencies, brand value is extremely difficult to measure, so branding campaigns can be easily defended with grandiose predictions of future glory.

Browser

An application used to view information from the Internet. Browsers provide a user-friendly interface for navigating through and accessing the vast amount of information on the Internet.

Click
The opportunity for a visitor to be transferred to a location by clicking on an ad, as recorded by the server.

Click-Through Rate
Percentage of times a user responded to an advertisement by clicking on the ad button/banner. At one time the granddaddy of Web-marketing measurements, click-through is based on the idea that online promotions that do what they're intended to do will elicit a click. CTR is one metric Internet marketers use to measure the performance of an ad campaign.

Code - Anything written in a language intended for computers to interpret.

Copyrighting
Copywriting for search engines is the art of creating web page copy that is tailored not only to fall in line with the current interpretation of search engine algorithms, but also to entice the reader to perform the action you desire. For example, to sign up for your newsletter, or click through to a certain area of your site.

Contextual Advertising
Advertising that is targeted to a Web page based on the page's content, keywords, or category. Ads in most content networks are targeted contextually.

Conversion Rate
This is the percentage of your clicks that generate sales or leads. This number is given by dividing the number of sale/leads by the number of clicks you send to the

offer. For example, if 100 clicks generated 100 visitors to your site, and they generate 5 sales/leads then your conversion rate would be 20%

Cookie
A file on your computer that records information such as where you have been on the World Wide Web. The browser stores this information which allows a site to remember the browser in future transactions or requests. Since the Web's protocol has no way to remember requests, cookies read and record a user's browser type and IP address, and store this information on the users own computer. The cookie can be read only by a server in the domain that stored it. Visitors can accept or deny cookies, by changing a setting in their browser preferences.

CPC
Cost Per Click. Also called Pay per Click (PPC). A performance-based advertising model where the advertiser pays a set fee for every click on an ad. The majority of text ads sold by search engines are billed under the CPC model.

CPC Campaign
A website marketing campaign based on a cost-per-click price where you only pay for the visitors that click on your listings. Hitwise Search Marketing provides guaranteed traffic at competitive cost per click prices. Due to our relationships with search engines combined with our optimization techniques, the price of marketing your website is lowered drastically.

CPL
Cost Per Lead

CPS
Cost Per Sale

CRM
Customer Relationship Management

CTA
Abbreviation for Content Targeted Advertising. It refers to the placement of relevant PPC ads on content pages for non-search engine websites.

CTR
Click Through Rate

Crawl - An automated, computerized algorithm hosted by search engines that browses the web. The programs create a copy of each webpage for future indexing by the search engines

Crawler
A program used by a search engine to "crawl" links on the Internet to find and index content. Also called a robot or spider. Can be used to identify and differentiate between types of crawlers indexing your site.

DNS - Domain Name System
Translates domain names to IP addresses. When a domain name is delegated to a name server, the domain name system ensures the name can be translated to the IP address of the web server.

Domain

A domain is the main subdivision of Internet addresses, the last three letters after the final dot, and it tells you what kind of organization you are dealing with. There are six top-level domains widely used: .com (commercial) .edu (educational),.net (network operations), .gov (US government), .mil (US military) and .org (organization). Other, two letter domains represent countries; thus;.uk for the United Kingdom, .dk for Denmark, .fr for France, .de for Germany, .es for Spain, .it for Italy and so on.

Email

Electronic Mail, text files that are sent from one person to another.

FAQ (Frequently Asked Questions)

FAQ is a commonly used abbreviation for "Frequently Asked Questions". Most Internet sites will have a "FAQ" to explain what is in the area and how to use its features.

Flash

A vector based animation program that has become a popular technology used to deliver content. Currently search engines have difficulty indexing flash effectively as robots cannot read the text that is held within.

Geo Targeting

Delivery of ads specific to the geographic location of the searcher. Geo-targeting allows the advertiser to specify where ads will or won't be shown based on the searcher's location, enabling more localized and personalized results.

Googlebot - The name of the spider used by Google. Instructions to Googlebot can be directed in the robots.txt file. Googlebot statistics can be viewed with web analytics software, on web server logs, and in Google webmaster tools.

Google Webmaster Tools - A webmaster resource that will help you with the crawling and indexing of your website.

Hacker
Originally used to describe a computer enthusiast who pushed a system to its highest performance through clever programming.

Hit
A hit is simply any request to the web server for any type of file. This can be an HTML page, an image (jpeg, gif, png, etc.), a sound clip, a cgi script, and many other file types. An HTML page can account for several hits: the page itself, each image on the page, and any embedded sound or video clips. Therefore, the number of hits a website receives is not a valid popularity gauge, but rather is an indication of server use and loading.

Home Page

The page designated as the main point of entry of a Web site (or main page) or the starting point when a browser first connects to the Internet. Typically, it welcomes you and introduces the purpose of the site, or the organization sponsoring it, and then provides links to the lower-level pages of the site. In business terms, it's the grabber. If your home page downloads too slowly, or it's unclear or uninteresting, you will probably lose a customer.

Host

An Internet host used to be a single machine connected to the Internet (which meant it had a unique IP address). As a host, it made available to other machines on the network certain services. However, virtual hosting has now meant that one physical host can now be actually many virtual hosts.

HTML

HyperTextMarkup Language is a coding language used to make hypertext documents for use on the Web. HTML resembles old-fashioned typesetting code, where a block of text is surrounded by codes that indicate how it should appear. HTML allows text to be "linked" to another file on the Internet.

HTTP

Hyper-Text Transfer Protocol, the format of the World Wide Web. When a browser sees "HTTP" at the beginning of an address, it knows that it is viewing a WWW page.

HTTPS
Hyper-Text Transfer Protocol Secure.

Hyperlink
This is the clickable link in text or graphics on a web page that takes you to another place on the same page, another page or a whole other site. It is the single most powerful and important function of online communications. Hyperlinks are revolutionizing the way the world gets its information.

Inbound Link
An inbound link is a hyperlink to a particular Web page from an outside site, bringing traffic to that Web page. Inbound links important because many search engine algorithms use the quality and quantity of inbound links to measure the popularity of a Web page.

Internet
A collection of approximately 60,000 independent, inter-connected networks that use the TCP/IP protocols and that evolved from ARPANet of the late '60s and early '70s. The Net," is a worldwide system of computer networks providing reliable and redundant connectivity between disparate computers and systems by using common transport and data protocols.

Internet Domain Name
The unique name that identifies an Internet entity.

Intranet

Intranets are private networks, usually maintained by corporations for internal communications, which use Internet – usually web – protocols, software and servers. They are relatively cheap, fast, and reliable networking and information warehouse systems that link offices around the world. They make it is easy for corporate users to communicate with one another, and to access the information resources of the Internet.

IP address

Internet Protocol address. Every system connected to the Internet has a unique IP address, which consists of a number in the format A.B.C.D where each of the four sections is a decimal number from 0 to 255. Most people use Domain Names instead and the resolution between Domain Names and IP addresses is handled by the network and the Domain Name Servers. With virtual hosting, a single machine can act like multiple machines (with multiple domain names and IP addresses).

Keyword

A word – or often phrase – used to focus an online search. A keyword is a database index entry that identifies a specific record or document. Keyword searching is the most common form of text search on the web. Most search engines do their text query and retrieval using keywords. Unless the author of the web document specifies the keywords for her document (this is possible by using meta tags), it's up to the search engine to determine them. Essentially, this means that search engines pull out and index words that are believed to be significant. Words that are mentioned towards the top of a document and words that are repeated several times throughout the document are more likely to be deemed important.

Keyword Matching - In Google Ad Words, there are four different keyword matching options, each specifying a different way for a keyword to interact with search queries. With some options, you'll enjoy more ad impressions; with others, you'll get fewer impressions (but potentially more targeted clicks). By applying the appropriate matching options to your keywords, you can best meet your ROI goals.
Your options are:

Broad Match - This is the default option. If your ad group contained the keyword tennis shoes, your ad would be eligible to appear when a user's search query contained tennis and shoes, in any order, and possibly along with other terms. Your ads could also show for singular/plural forms, synonyms, and other relevant variations. For example, you ad might show on tennis shoe or tennis sneakers. Run a Search Query Performance Report to see what keyword variations trigger your ad.

Phrase Match - If you enter your keyword in quotation marks, as in "tennis shoes," your ad would be eligible to appear when a user searches on the phrase tennis shoes, in this order, and possibly with other terms before or after the phrase. For example, your ad could appear for the query red tennis shoes but not for shoes for tennis, tennis shoe, or tennis sneakers. Phrase match is more targeted than broad match, but more flexible than exact match.

Exact Match - If you surround your keywords in brackets - such as [tennis shoes] - your ad would be eligible to appear when a user searches for the specific phrase tennis shoes, in this order, and without any other terms in the query. For example, your ad wouldn't show for the query red tennis shoes or tennis shoe. Exact match is the most targeted option. Although you won't receive as many impressions with exact match, you'll likely enjoy the most targeted clicks - users searching for your exact keyword typically want precisely what your business has to offer.

Negative Keyword - If your keyword is tennis shoes and you add the negative keyword -red, your ad will not appear when a user searches on red tennis shoes. Negative keywords are especially useful if your account contains lots of broad-matched keywords. It's a good idea to add any irrelevant keyword variations you see in a Search Query Performance Report or the Keyword Tool as a negative keyword.

Remember, no matter which matching options you use, it's important to only use keywords that accurately describe your product or service.

Keyword Audit
independent third-party verification of your keyword use, strategy, bidding, and return on investment.

Keyword Bidding

Keyword Bidding is the process or method used by search engines marketers to determine the ranking of paid keywords results in AOL, Google, MSN, Yahoo, and other search engines that require pay per click advertising to determine your ranking and positioning in their search results and in content results on networked partners' sites.

Keyword Research
Keyword research includes the processes and methodologies to research key words that would be used for search and internet marketing campaigns.

Keyword Marketing
Keyword Marketing is the act, process, or technique of promoting, selling, and distributing a product or service on-line.

Link
An electronic connection between two Web sites (also called "hot link").

Link Building
The process of getting quality Web sites to link to your Web site, in order to improve search engine rankings. Link building techniques can reciprocal linking, entering barter arrangements, and may include buying links.

Link Popularity
A measure of inbound links. Several search engines have included this factor into their algorithms, the

most notable being Goggle with their trademarked PageRank.

Mailing List
Online a mailing list is an automatically distributed email message on a particular topics going to certain individuals. You can subscribe or unsubscribe to a mailing list by sending a message via email. There are many good professional mailing lists, and you should find the ones that concern your business.

Meta Data
Data about Data. Examples are the Meta Tags in a HTML page.

My Space
MySpace is a social networking website offering an interactive, user-generated content with network of friends, music, photos, bulletins, blogs, groups, and more.

Opt in/Opt out
An email marketing promotion that typically gives consumers an opportunity to "opt in" (taking action to be part of the promotion) or to "opt out" (taking action to not be part of the promotion). Marketers can be sensitive about the distinction, although many are secretly anxious about the day when email, like real-world direct mail, becomes an opt-out medium.

Page
All Web sites are a collection of electronic "pages." Each Web page is a document formatted in HTML

(Hypertext Markup Language) that contains text, images or media objects such as RealAudio player files, QuickTime videos or Java applets. The "home page" is typically a visitor's first point of entry and features a site index. Pages can be static or dynamically generated. All frames and frame parent documents are counted as pages.

Page Request
The opportunity for an HTML document to be appear in a browser window as a direct result of a visitors interaction with a Web site (IAB). The page request is for a browser to "get' a page from a site and this request is recorded by the server log.

Page Views
Number of times a user requests a page that may contain a particular ad. A page is defined as any file or content delivered by a web server that would generally be considered a web document. This includes HTML pages (.html, .htm, .shtml), script-generated pages (.cgi, .asp, .cfm, etc.), and plain-text pages. It also includes sound files (.wav, .aiff, etc.), video files (.mov, etc.), and other non-document files. Only image files (.jpeg, .gif, .png), javascript (.js) and style sheets (.css) are excluded from this definition.

Pay-per-Click
An advertising pricing model in which advertisers pay agencies based on how many consumers clicked on a promotion. Condemned by advertisers and agencies alike for its many marketing vagaries and technical loopholes.

Pay-per-Impression
An advertising pricing model in which advertisers pay agencies based on how many consumers see their promotions.

Pay-per-Sale
An advertising pricing model in which advertisers pay agencies based on how many consumers actually buy something as a direct result of the promotion. Despised by agencies for the wretched accountability it brings to their lives.

PDF
Portable Document Format. Word processing software, business applications or desktop publishing files on the Web that look exactly like the originals. Must have Adobe Acrobat Reader to view.

PDF Files
Adobe's Portable Document Format (pdf) is a translation format used primarily for distributing files across a network, or on a web site. Files with a .pdf extension have been created in another application and then translated into .pdf files so they can be viewed by anyone – regardless of platform.

PPC
Pay Per Click. A type of campaign or service which applies a CPC price to relevant keyword phrases to easily and accurately calculate positioning, online marketing costs and ROI for your website. As opposed to a

Maintenance or Optimization SEO campaign, the client only pays for the traffic that is provided, based on the agreed CPC.

PPC Management
The process of managing PPC accounts, campaigns, ad groups, and keywords.

Podcast
A method of publishing audio files to the Internet for playback on mobile devices and personal computers.

Portal
A Web site or service that offers a broad array of resources and services, such as email, forums, search engines, and on-line shopping malls. The first Web portals were online services, such as AOL, that provided access to the Web, but by now most of the traditional search engines have transformed themselves into Web portals to attract and keep a larger audience. Also known as a "gateway to the Internet".

Query
A request for information, usually to a search engine. A key word or phrase that instructs the search engine to find documents related to the user's request.

Quality Score
A score assigned by search engines that is calculated by measuring an ad's click through rate, analyzing the relevance of the landing page, and considering other factors used to determine the quality of a site and re-

ward those of higher quality with top placement and lower bid requirements. Some factors that make up a quality score are historical keyword performance, the quality of an ad's landing page, and other undisclosed attributes. All of the major search engines now use some form of quality score in their search ad algorithm.

Rank

An ad's standing in comparison to other ads, based on the graphical click-through rate. Rank provides advertisers with information on an ad's performance across sites.

Referrer

The URL or webpage that the user clicked on to arrive at your web page. This is often recorded in the log files via the web server software.

Robot

See spider or crawler.

Robots.txt

A file place on your website directory tree which gives instructions to robots/spiders as to what content to access.

ROI

Return on investment = (Revenue - Cost)/ Cost, expressed as a percentage. A term describing the calculation of the financial return on an Internet marketing or advertising initiative that incurs some cost. Determining ROI and the actual ROI in Internet marketing and advertising has been much more accurate than television, radio, and traditional media.

Search Advertising
An advertiser pays for the chance to have their ad display when a user searches for a given keyword. These are usually text ads, which are displayed above or to the right of the algorithmic (organic) search results. Most search ads are sold by the PPC model, where the advertiser pays only when the user clicks on the ad or text link.

Search Engine
A program that searches documents for specified keywords and returns a list of the documents where the keywords were found. Although search engine is really a general class of programs, the term is often used to specifically describe systems like Google, Yahoo and Bing that enable users to search for documents on the World Wide Web.

SEM - Search Engine Marketing
The process of building and marketing a site with the goal of improving its position in search engine results. SEM includes search engine optimization (SEO) and pay per click advertising (PPC), as well as using all other areas and services offered by Search Engines.

Search Terms
Text that is typed into a search engine to gain results leading to related content.

SEO
Search Engine Optimization is the ongoing process of making a site and its content highly relevant for both search engines and searchers. SEO includes technical tasks to make it easier for search engines to find and index a site for the appropriate keywords, as well as marketing-focused tasks to make a site more appealing to users. Successful search marketing helps a site gain top positioning for relevant words and phrases.

SEO Services
SEO Services are designed to get your website a top ranking in the results of search engines for any given keyword.

SER
Search Engine Results

SERP
Search Engine Results Page. The page searchers see after they've entered their query into the search box. This page lists several Web pages related to the searcher's query, sorted by relevance. Increasingly, search engines are returning blended search results, which include images, videos, and results from specialty databases on their SERPs.

Shareware
Software programs that are openly available, and usually they can be downloaded online. They are often free, though not always.

Social Media
A category of sites that is based on user participation and user-generated content. They include social networking sites like LinkedIn, Facebook, or My Space, social bookmarking sites like Del.icio.us, social news sites like Digg or Simpy, and other sites that are centered on user interaction.

Spam
The use of mailing lists to blanket usenets or private email boxes with indiscriminate advertising messages. Very bad netiquette. Even worse, it's bad business. The future of marketing online is about customizing products and information for individual users. Anyone who tries to use old mass market techniques in the new media environment is bound to fail.

Spider (Robot)
A term used to describe search engines such as Google, Yahoo and Bing, because of the way they cruise all over the world wide web to find information. It is a software program which combs the web for new sites and updated information on old ones, like a spider looking for a fly.

Standard Match Type
An option within Sponsored Search that specifies how search terms are matched to ads. Ads that use the standard match type are displayed for exact matches to your keywords, as well as for singular or plural variations and common misspellings.

Stickiness

A measure used to gauge the effectiveness of a site in retaining individual users. The term is typically used in promotional material when traffic numbers are too low to be effective in lauding a site's performance. Never mind the quantity, feel the stick.

Surfing

Exploring World Wide Web. Commonly seen as "Surfing the 'Net."

Tags

Individual keywords or phrases for organizing content

Targeted Marketing

Banners or other promotions aimed, on the basis of demographic analysis, at one specific subsection of the market.

Title

An element of a web page which appears in the top left of most browsers. It is also the part of a directory submission that represents the title of the website. Arguably one of the most important parts of SEO is ensuring an optimized title or unique titles across all pages of a website.

Tracking Domain

A domain specifically created to measure traffic delivered to a website.

Traffic

Generally measured by the amount of visitors to a website. Hitwise Search Marketing measures search generated traffic separately by recording referrals from known search engines and directories.

Unique Users
The total number of different users, or different computer terminals which have visited a Web site. This is measured using advanced tracking technology or user registration.

Upload
To send a file from one computer to another via modem or other telecommunication method.

URL
Uniform Resource Locator, an HTTP address used by the World Wide Web to specify a certain site. This is the unique identifier, or address, of a web page on the Internet. URL can be pronounced "you-are-ell" or "earl." It is how web pages, ftp's, gophers, newsgroups and even some email boxes are located.

Valid Hits
A further refinement of hits, valid hits are hits that deliver all information to a user. Excludes hits such as redirects, error messages and computer-generated hits.

Viral Marketing
Any advertising that propagates itself. When Hotmail users send email, they unwittingly infect the recipient with the tag line at the bottom of the message.

Virus

These are programs that can be downloaded onto your computer or network from the Internet. Some are harmless, others are programmed to destroy your system, trash your files and disable your software. No kidding. So be careful. Use anti-virus programs. They take a few extra minutes every day to use, but the protection is worth it.

Vlog

A vlog is a video blog.

Visits

A sequence of requests made by one user at one site. If a visitor does not request any new information for a period of time, known as the "time-out" period, then the next request by the visitor is considered a new visit. To enable comparisons among sites, I/PRO uses a 30-minute time-out.

W3/ W3C

World Wide Web Consortium. The W3C, or World Wide Web Consortium, is a standards body dedicated to ensuring interoperability between all the varied system and network types that comprise the World Wide Web part of the Internet. The W3C log format is commonly used by several web server software systems, such as Microsoft IIS.

Web 2.0
A term that refers to a second generation of Internet-based services. These usually include tools that let people collaborate and share information online, such as social networking sites, wikis, communication tools, and folksonomies.

Web page
A HTML (Hypertext mark-up Language) document on the web, usually one of many together that make up a web site.

Webmaster
The individual assigned to administering a corporation or organization's web site. This person lays out the information trees, designs the look, codes HTML pages, handles editing and additions and checks that links are intact. In addition, he or she monitors, routes and sometimes responds to email generated by the site

Web Site
The virtual location for an organization's presence on the World Wide Web, usually making up several web pages and a single home page designated by a unique URL.

Wikipedia - A multilingual, web-based, free content encyclopaedia project. Wikipedia is written collaboratively by volunteers from all around the world. With rare exceptions, its articles can be edited by anyone with access to the Internet, simply by clicking the edit this page link. Since its creation in 2001, the name

Wikipedia is a portmanteau of the words wiki (a type of collaborative website) and encyclopaedia.

Wiki - A web application that allows users to add content, as on an Internet forum, but also allows anyone to edit the content. Wiki also refers to the collaborative software used to create such a website

World Wide Web

The web allows computer users to access information across systems around the world using URLs to identify files and systems and hypertext links to move between files on the same or different systems. The web is a client/server information system that supports the retrieval of data in the form of text, graphics and multimedia in a uniform HTML format. Allowing hypertext links and interactivity on an unprecedented level, its introduction transformed a sleepy, academic communications system into a powerful marketing tool linking businesses and customers around the world.